AIR CAMPAIGN

OPERATION *BARBAROSSA* 1941
The Luftwaffe opens the Eastern Front campaign

WILLIAM E. HIESTAND | ILLUSTRATED BY MADS BANGSØ

OSPREY PUBLISHING
Bloomsbury Publishing Plc
Kemp House, Chawley Park, Cumnor Hill, Oxford OX2 9PH, UK
29 Earlsfort Terrace, Dublin 2, Ireland
1385 Broadway, 5th Floor, New York, NY 10018, USA
E-mail: info@ospreypublishing.com
www.ospreypublishing.com

OSPREY is a trademark of Osprey Publishing Ltd

First published in Great Britain in 2024

© Osprey Publishing Ltd, 2024

All rights reserved. No part of this publication may be reproduced or transmitted in any form or by any means, electronic or mechanical, including photocopying, recording, or any information storage or retrieval system, without prior permission in writing from the publishers.

A catalog record for this book is available from the British Library.

ISBN: PB 9781472861504; eBook 9781472861511;
ePDF 9781472861528; XML 9781472861498

24 25 26 27 28 10 9 8 7 6 5 4 3 2 1

Maps by www.bounford.com
Diagrams by Adam Tooby
3D BEVs by Paul Kime
Index by Fionbar Lyons
Typeset by PDQ Digital Media Solutions, Bungay, UK
Printed and bound in India by Replika Press Private Ltd.

Title page: Luftwaffe He 111 delivering its bomb load. Operation *Barbarossa* would see the Luftwaffe hard-pressed as it strained to support widely divergent ground operations on a vast front. (WH 2529 Nik Cornish)

Osprey Publishing supports the Woodland Trust, the UK's leading woodland conservation charity.

To find out more about our authors and books visit www.ospreypublishing.com. Here you will find extracts, author interviews, details of forthcoming events and the option to sign up for our newsletter.

German forces
Fliegerkorps: Air Corps
Geschwader: Air Wing
Gruppe: Air Group
Heer: Army
JG: Fighter Wing
KG: Bomber Wing
Landser: Infantryman
Luftflotte: Air Fleet
OKH: *Oberkommando des Heeres*
OKL: *Oberkommando der Luftwaffe*
SKG: Fast Attack Bomber Wing
Staffel: Squadron
StG: Stuka Dive-Bomber Wing (*Sturzkampfgeschwader*)
ZG: Destroyer Wing

Soviet forces
BABr: Bomber Aviation Brigade
BAD: Bomber Aviation Division
BAK: Long-Range Bomber Aviation Corps
BAP: Bomber Aviation Regiment
DBA: Long-Range Bomber Aviation
DBAD: Long-Range Bomber Aviation Division
DBAP: Long-Range Bomber Aviation Regiment
GVF: Civil Air Fleet
IAD: Fighter Aviation Division
IAK: Fighter Aviation Corps
IAP: Fighter Aviation Regiment
MTAP: Mine and Torpedo Aviation Regiment
NKVD: People's Commissariat for Internal Affairs
PVO: Homeland Air Defense
SBAP: High-Speed Bomber Aviation Regiment
ShAP: Ground Attack Aviation Regiment
SAD: Mixed (Composite) Aviation Division
Stavka: Supreme High Command
TBAP: Heavy Bomber Aviation Regiment
VVS: Military Air Force
VVS-VMF: Naval Air Force

AIR CAMPAIGN

CONTENTS

CONTENTS	3
INTRODUCTION	4
ATTACKER'S CAPABILITIES	10
DEFENDER'S CAPABILITIES	19
CAMPAIGN OBJECTIVES	31
THE CAMPAIGN	34
AFTERMATH AND ANALYSIS	87
FURTHER READING	93
INDEX	95

INTRODUCTION

The Soviet air forces were in the midst of a major modernization program when caught on the ground by the Luftwaffe's June 22 attack. The majority of its force was made up of obsolete types such as the I-16 Ishak ("Donkey") fighter. (Courtesy of the Central Museum of the Armed Forces, Moscow via Stavka)

The Luftwaffe's surprise attack on the Soviet Military Air Force (VVS) in the early morning hours of June 22, 1941, was the single most devastating air operation in history. As part of Nazi Germany's Operation *Barbarossa*, Hitler's Luftwaffe – a force at the peak of its powers – destroyed over a thousand enemy aircraft, most of them caught parked wingtip-to-wingtip at their bases. Stalin's airmen responded throughout the day with as many as 6,000 sorties, but they suffered hundreds of losses in the air to the veteran Luftwaffe fighter pilots in their Bf 109s. Soviet pilots fought with desperate courage, some sacrificing their own aircraft and often their lives by ramming German bombers when out of ammunition, but the Wehrmacht rapidly drove deep into the USSR. The remaining months of 1941 saw one of the largest and most intensive sustained air campaigns of the war, with the VVS and Red Army continuing to battle for survival and the Luftwaffe straining to support offensives over a 2,500km (1,553-mile) front stretching from the Arctic Circle to the Crimea and Black Sea.

As over Poland and France, the Luftwaffe sought to destroy the enemy air force on the ground, seize air superiority, and support the panzer groups' deep advances by smashing enemy defenses and cutting their lines of communication. The Red Air Force's devastating losses forced it to draw reinforcements from training units, military districts in the central and eastern USSR, and field hastily formed new regiments. The *Barbarossa* air campaign was fought in widely varying weather conditions ranging from high summer, through fall rains and into the subzero Eurasian winter. Air operations included strategic bombing, maritime mining and strikes, and support to amphibious operations in addition to the high-intensity air-to-air and air-to-ground combat on the main front. By December 1941, the exhausted German Heer and Luftwaffe ground to a halt at the gates of Moscow, Leningrad, and Rostov. Stalin's regime and his army and air forces had survived the massive defeats of 1941, and the Luftwaffe, trained and organized for short, decisive campaigns, found itself locked in an attritional war that would end in its ultimate defeat.

Origins

Unable to drive Britain out of the war in the summer of 1940, Hitler turned to his primary geostrategic ambition: the destruction of the Soviet Union. On December 18, he issued Führer Directive No. 21, ordering the Wehrmacht to prepare to defeat Stalin's regime in a rapid, six-week campaign. The senior officer corps, flush with Germany's swift successes in a series of campaigns under the Führer's leadership, largely ignored planning concerns with distance, logistics, and the defensive potential of Soviet forces. Formal Luftwaffe planning for Operation *Barbarossa* began in January 1941.

Hitler ordered a program of high-altitude reconnaissance flights of up to 300km (186 miles) deep into Soviet territory to prepare for *Barbarossa*. The Luftwaffe's specialized high-altitude reconnaissance unit, Oberst Theodor Rowehl's *Aufklärungsgruppe ObdL* (Reconnaissance Group of the Luftwaffe High Command), began operations with He 111s with special high-altitude engines, Ju 86Ps with extended wings and pressurized cabins, Do 215s, and Ju 88s. The German aircraft operated at 9,000–12,000m (30,000–40,000ft), too high for Soviet fighters to intercept, and photographed a variety of targets including troop concentrations, headquarters, rail terminals, and in particular airfields. Two of the VVS's new MiG-3 fighters stalled and crashed after trying to intercept one of Rowehl's aircraft over the Baltic States on April 10, but Stalin, fearing any measures that could provoke a military escalation, ordered no action against the flights except an "invitation to land." One Ju 86P was forced down near Vinnitsa by poor weather on April 15, but Stalin remained determined to avoid responding to "provocations" despite the film of Soviet facilities in the crashed aircraft. The German photographic intelligence effort was complemented by ongoing signals collection from a series of weather stations in eastern Europe, expanded after 1939 into Finland, Hungary, and Romania. By June 21, Rowehl's airmen had flown over 500 reconnaissance missions, and although German intelligence underestimated the Soviet Union's overall defensive potential, the Luftwaffe was able to effectively target the airbase network in the western USSR. Some of the last flights in the hours before the invasion delivered agents to seize bridges and cut Soviet wire communications.

A Stuka delivering a bomb, 1941. (Getty Images)

Luftwaffe aircraft began displacing to their combat airfields in the East in May. Despite the reconnaissance flights and the buildup in Poland, Stalin prohibited camouflage or dispersal activities at VVS airfields. The Soviet dictator dismissed warnings from Western allies as efforts to trick the USSR into the war against the Nazis, and similarly rejected warnings from the *Rote Kapelle* (Red Chapel) spy network of anti-Nazi sympathizers. By mid-June, evidence of the German buildup became more difficult to ignore and Stalin permitted halting preparations. On June 18, Homeland Air Defense (PVO) antiaircraft units were told to prepare for an alert in three days' time, and the next day the Stavka issued orders to begin camouflage operations at airfields. People's Commissar for Defense Marshal Semyon Timoshenko convinced Stalin in the early morning hours of June 22 that an attack was imminent, and Moscow finally issued an alert order to the border military districts. Problems with communications meant that few units received the order in time, and in the Western Special Military District, only one of General Ivan Kopet's six divisions, the 10 Mixed Aviation Division (SAD), received the order before the attack. Some VVS officers were only handed the message – complete with admonitions not to respond to "provocations" or shoot down enemy aircraft – as they stood among their burning aircraft.

CHRONOLOGY

1940

Late 1940–May 1941 The Luftwaffe conducts a sustained program of high-altitude reconnaissance flights over the western USSR.

December 18, 1940 Hitler issues Directive No. 21 for Operation *Barbarossa*. The Luftwaffe will support the ground forces in a rapid, six-week campaign to destroy the Soviet regime and occupy the western USSR while continuing operations in the Atlantic, Mediterranean, and against Britain.

1941

January 13 The Luftwaffe begins preliminary planning for *Barbarossa*. Göring establishes a planning staff on February 20.

April 6 The German campaign in the Balkans begins.

April 15 A Ju 86P of the Luftwaffe high-altitude reconnaissance unit, *Aufklärungsgruppe ObdL*, crashes near Rovno, but although photographs of Soviet facilities are found in the aircraft's cameras, Stalin forbids any action be taken.

June 14 Hitler affirms that German objectives for *Barbarossa* are Leningrad, the Ukraine, the Donbas, and the oilfields of the Caucasus.

June 22 *Barbarossatag* (*Barbarossa* Day). Massive surprise Luftwaffe attacks against Soviet airfields begin around 0330–0400hrs. With the onset of hostilities, the Soviet Baltic, Western, Kiev, and Odessa Special Military Districts on the border are redesignated as the Northwestern, Western, Southern, and Southwestern Fronts. As many as 1,500 aircraft are destroyed on the ground during the first day. The Soviets manage to fly an estimated 6,000 sorties on June 22, but the unescorted VVS bomber squadrons attempting to attack the panzer spearheads take massive losses, as do the long-range bombers of DBA when ordered into action later in the day.

June 22–30 The Soviet garrison in the fortress of Brest is bypassed by General Heinz Guderian's Panzer Group 2, but holds out despite repeated attacks by the German 45 Infantry Division. Ultimately, the Luftwaffe shatters the fortress walls with heavy bombs.

June 23–30 The Soviet Northwestern, Western, and Southwestern Fronts launch attacks with their reserve mechanized corps leading to some of the largest tank clashes in history. The VVS frontal and DBA bomber force attempting to support the attacks suffer more heavy losses to German flak and the veteran Bf 109 pilots. The Luftwaffe throws all available aircraft against the attackers and plays a major role in shattering the Soviet mechanized columns.

June 23–October 15 The Soviet launch small-scale raids against port facilities and oil infrastructure targets in Romania, using a mix of VVS, DBA, and Naval assets.

LTC Theodor Rowehl founded the Luftwaffe's high-altitude reconnaissance capability in the 1930s, and in 1940–41 led the *Aufklärungsgruppe ObdL* in extensive photo-reconnaissance surveys of Soviet military facilities in the western USSR, with particular attention paid to airfields. Stalin prohibited any attempts to shoot down the intruding German aircraft. (Getty Images)

June 24–25 The Luftwaffe begins to shift from raids on VVS airfields to ground force support and attacks on Soviet lines of communication.

June 26 Soviet Northern Front VVS bombers under the aggressive General Alexander Novikov launch preemptive strikes against German aircraft on Finnish airfields. Along with reported artillery strikes, the air attacks give Helsinki a rationale to join in the offensive. On June 29, Mountain Corps Norway launches its attack towards Murmansk, supported by elements of Luftflotte 5 stationed in Norway.

June 27 Three aircraft identified as Soviet bomb the city of Kassa in Hungary, bringing Budapest into the war against the USSR.

June 28–29 Guderian and Hoth encircle the bulk of the Western Front around Białystok and Minsk. General der Flieger Wolfram von Richthofen's Fliegerkorps VIII, the Luftwaffe's preeminent ground-support organization, provides Hoth with strong air support, while Guderian complains about General der Flieger Bruno Loerzer's Fliegerkorps II. The Luftwaffe is already facing the challenge of having too few units and aircraft to meet the needs of the army on an ever-widening front.

June 30 In the first six days of the war, the Germans claim to have destroyed 3,100 aircraft and the Soviets report 3,922 lost. The Luftwaffe has lost 684 aircraft destroyed or severely damaged, 484 of them to enemy action.

July Led by Panzer Group 4, Army Group North drives into the Baltic States. With the VVS Northwestern Front shattered, the Soviets draw on the aviation forces of the Baltic Fleet and Novikov's VVS Northern Front to combat the German advance.

July 10 The Stavka creates the Northwestern, Western, and Southwestern Strategic Direction commands under Marshals Voroshilov, Timoshenko, and Budennyy to improve control of the various fronts. Each Strategic Direction has a VVS commander: Novikov for the Northwestern, Colonel N.F. Naumenko for the Western, and General F. Ya Falaleyev for the Southern.

July 11 The Białystok and Minsk pockets are destroyed, but as Panzer Groups 2 and 3 continue their advance east, they encounter new Soviet reserve armies assembling to defend the Smolensk area.

July 14–18 The Soviet 11th Army with VVS air support counterattacks Army Group North's lead elements at Soltsy, delaying the German advance.

July 15 The Soviets reduce VVS regimental strengths from 64 to 32 aircraft due to losses, and to make the units easier to control.

July 16 Army Group Center penetrates Soviet defenses in the Smolensk area, and Guderian's Panzer Group 2 takes the city, meeting Hoth's Panzer Group 3 to form a new pocket. The VVS supports counterattacks by the Western Front that allow roughly 100,000 Soviet troops to escape the encirclement.

July 19 Hitler orders resources shifted from Army Group Center to aid the offensives to the north and south. The Luftwaffe is ordered to destroy Moscow from the air.

July 21–22 195 Luftwaffe bombers launch their first and largest raid on Moscow, dispatching 195 bombers, followed over the next two nights by additional raids of 115 and 125. Demands for air support at the front lead to a shift to smaller-scale raids, often of three to ten bombers, that continue into 1942.

July 23–August 7 The Soviet Western Front begins a series of counteroffensives against Army Group Center.

July 30 OKW Directive No. 34 directs Army Group North to attack Leningrad and establish contact with the Finns, and Richthofen's Fliegerkorps VIII is shifted north to support a renewed attack on August 6. General der Flieger Richthofen takes 9 Gruppen (293 aircraft), leaving Generalfeldmarschall Albert Kesselring with 19 Gruppen (600 aircraft) in Fliegerkorps II to support Army Group Center.

August 3–8 After defeating the Southwestern Front's mechanized counterattacks, von Rundstedt's Army Group South attacks into the Ukraine in July. With the direct approach against Kiev slowed by VVS and Red Army resistance, von Rundstedt shifts to the southeast, and on August 3, German forces close a pocket around Uman. The Luftwaffe defeats Soviet relief attempts, and the pocket is destroyed on August 8.

August 7–8 The Soviets launch the first raid on Berlin, with five of 15 Baltic Fleet DB-3T bombers reaching the city center and dropping 30 100kg (220lb) bombs. The Baltic Fleet and DBA launch nine additional raids

A Stuka orbits over an assault gun during the advance into the USSR. Although a separate service, the Luftwaffe worked closely with its army counterparts. After destroying enemy air forces on the ground, German air operations focused on isolating the battlefield by interdiction attacks and providing close support to the advancing panzer groups. (Getty Images)

with a total of 54 bombers before German amphibious operations against the Baltic Islands used as staging bases end the operations in early September.

August 8–October 15 Romanian forces besiege the Soviet Coastal Army in Odessa. The VVS 69 Regiment and VVS Black Sea Fleet forces inflict heavy losses on the Romanian air element, and Romanian ground forces are repulsed in a series of unsuccessful ground assaults. Soviet forces withdraw by sea to Sevastopol on October 15 with few losses.

August 9–24 The Smolensk pocket is destroyed, and the Soviets launch a major offensive against Army Group Center's positions in the Yelnya Salient, retaking the city on September 6.

August 22 Hitler ends the debate about objectives with his high command and directs Panzer Group 2 and 2 Army to strike south and encircle Kirponos's Southwestern Front, which is defending Kiev and the eastern Ukraine. Guderian's Panzer Group begins to attack to the south the next day, supported by elements of Loerzer's Fliegerkorps II.

Late August–early September Luftwaffe forces repel a Soviet air offensive organized by the Stavka high command and launched by the reinforced VVS Bryansk Front against Guderian's long left flank.

September 8 Supported by Richthofen's expert Fliegerkorps VIII ground-support airmen, Army Group North isolates Leningrad with the capture of the Shlisselburg Fortress on the shores of Lake Ladoga. Generaloberst Albert Keller's bombers launch the first major raid on the city the same day, destroying the warehouses holding the city's food reserves with incendiaries.

September 14 Panzer Groups 1 and 2 link up, encircling the Southwestern Front in a massive pocket. Kiev falls five days later, and the pocket is destroyed on September 24. In the Baltic, German forces begin amphibious operations against the Baltic Islands, and the VVS Baltic Fleet and DBA bombers are no longer able to use them as staging areas for strikes on Berlin.

September 15 Richthofen's Fliegerkorps VIII returns to Army Group Center to prepare for Operation *Typhoon* against Moscow.

September 20–24 Army Group North retains the Stukas of StG 2 for strikes against the Baltic Fleet in Kronstadt. Despite defensive operations by 40 navy fighters, the Stukas achieve a number of hits on Soviet naval units. When the 250kg (551lb) and 500kg (1,102lb) bombs fail to sink their targets, Stuka ace Hans-Ulrich Rudel sinks the battleship Marat on September 21 using one-ton armor-piercing bombs.

September 22 Hitler orders Leningrad to be starved and the siege lines solidify September 25. The Luftwaffe will launch an ongoing series of strikes against the city and Soviet supply lines over Lake Ladoga.

September 30–October 2 Army Group Center begins Operation *Typhoon*.

October 3 Stavka orders the 5th Airborne Corps airlifted into Orel, but the city soon falls to Guderian's panzers.

October 5 Panzer Groups 1, 2, and 3 are redesignated Panzer Armies.

Hungarian fighters in action over the front in summer/autumn 1941. (Getty Images)

October 7 The Germans close a massive pocket around Vyazma, and another is closed around Bryansk the next day. VVS units are rushed to the Moscow front to help plug the huge gap torn in Soviet lines, and the fall rains begin to turn the fields and roads to mud, bringing the German advance to a halt. Judging the Soviets to be finished, 16 of 29 Gruppen in Luftwaffe 2 are ordered to transfer to Germany or other theaters. Kesselring's Luftflotte 2 and Fliegerkorps II headquarters depart in November to begin operations against Malta. Generaloberst Alexander Loehr also loses the Fliegerkorps V headquarters under Ritter von Greim, which is ordered to Brussels to begin organizing a Luftwaffe aerial mining formation.

October 24 Army Group South takes Kharkov, but its advance against the city was severely delayed by VVS strikes, allowing the USSR to evacuate critical war industries from Kharkov and other Donbas cities. Von Rundstedt's troops begin the advance to take the Crimea, Sevastopol, Rostov, Stalingrad, and Maikop.

November Army Group Center renews its attack on the now-frozen ground. Unlike the army, the Luftwaffe has been provided with winter clothing, but it faces major challenges as units leave for other theaters, and the remaining units struggle to operate in the severe cold. While the Luftwaffe flies from primitive airfields, the VVS can use the well-equipped airbase network around Moscow.

November 8 Army Group North takes Tikhvin, cutting the rail network supporting communications with Leningrad, but Soviet counterattacks force German forces to retreat from the city on December 7.

November 15–22 Army Group Center makes progress over the frozen terrain, with advances to the north and south threatening to encircle Moscow.

November 20 German forces take Rostov but withdraw nine days later. Von Rundstedt resigns November 30.

December 4–5 The German offensive grinds to a halt in the extreme cold and in the face of intense Soviet resistance.

December 5 The Kalinin Front begins the Soviet Winter Counteroffensive, and Zhukov's Western Front attacks the next day.

The mainstay of the Luftwaffe medium bomber force was the Heinkel He 111. The pressures of the conflict with the Soviet Union would force the bomber force to repeatedly be used for low-level close support operations, leading to numbers of He 111s being heavily damaged by or lost to enemy ground fire. (Nik Cornish at www.stavka.photos/)

ATTACKER'S CAPABILITIES

The Luftwaffe at its peak

Nazi Germany committed close to 3,000 combat aircraft to the offensive, and its allies contributed another 1,000. The Luftwaffe's overall strength had not increased significantly since the offensive against France in 1940, and in mid-1941 the need to support operations in other theaters meant roughly 60 percent of the force was available for *Barbarossa*. While the ground forces of Germany and its allies began the assault with 3.5 million men, outnumbering the 2.3 million Soviet troops in the border military districts, the situation was reversed in the air, with almost 10,000 Soviet combat aircraft in the western USSR outnumbering their Axis attackers by a margin of over two to one. The Luftwaffe was at the height of its capabilities in June 1941, however, and with superior aircraft, proven doctrine, and veteran pilots and personnel, it would inflict devastating losses on its Soviet opponents.

Command and control

Air force Commander-in-Chief Hermann Göring ensured that, apart from tactical reconnaissance aircraft attached to ground armies, all combat aviation resources were controlled by the Luftwaffe. Although the force was supremely effective at the tactical and operational levels, strategic guidance suffered due to Göring's indolence and short attention span. Tensions between senior leaders Chief of Staff Han Jeschonnek, Inspector General Erhard Milch, and Luftwaffe *Generalluftzeugmeister* (Chief of Procurement and Supply) Ernst Udet further complicated high-level decision making. The Luftwaffe lacked a true service General Staff like the Heer's OKH and the Kriegsmarine's OKM and, as Jeschonnek's OKL (*Oberkommando der Luftwaffe*) operated more as Göring's personal staff, most of the operational planning was left to the Luftflotten and Fliegerkorps. Milch was an experienced and capable organizer and manager who had served as the head of Lufthansa, but Udet was out of his depth as head of aircraft design. Both Udet and Jeschonnek would commit suicide, Udet in November 1941 and Jeschonnek in August 1943.

Dornier Do 17 bombers from *Kampfgruppe* (KG) 2 flying over the Acropolis in Athens. Richthofen's Fliegerkorps VIII was heavily engaged in the Balkan Campaign in the weeks before Operation *Barbarossa*. The invasion of the Soviet Union saw the last operational use of the Do 17, which was in the process of being replaced by the more capable Ju 88. (Getty Images)

The Luftwaffe brought its combat-proven doctrine for air operations to *Barbarossa*. As in Poland and France, the German airmen would first deliver sustained attacks against the enemy's airbases to gain air superiority (*luftüberlegenheit*). With opposition eliminated, the Luftwaffe would turn to the support of ground force operations both with direct army support (*unmittelbare Heeresunterstuetzung*) to break through lines of resistance, and operational-level attacks against targets deeper behind the frontline. These indirect army support operations (*mittelbare Heeresunterstuetzung*) were primarily focused on enemy line of communications targets such as roads, bridges, and the rail network, but could include other relevant targets including depots, headquarters, troop concentrations, and even select industrial targets.

While Göring kept the Luftwaffe independent, its staff had years of combat experience working closely with ground force staff at the army group and army levels to plan and coordinate operations, including daily priorities for targets and airstrikes. The Luftwaffe's efficient radio network allowed its leaders to closely monitor operations and rapidly shift air units around the battlefront as needed. Airfield and logistical elements were trained to displace forward quickly to keep up with the advancing ground troops, although the vast distances, primitive lines of communications, and field airstrips encountered in the Soviet Union soon reduced aircraft readiness levels.

Luftwaffe bombing of Factory 22, which produced Tupolev and Ilyushin heavy bombers, in the Moscow suburb of Fili, August 5, 1941. Most Luftwaffe raids against the capital were conducted at night to reduce losses. (Nik Cornish T 82)

The Luftwaffe assigned Flivo (*Fliegerverbindungsoffizier*) liaison officers to army group, corps, and panzer and motorized division headquarters to ensure continuous air support to the ground scheme of maneuver. Requests from the troops for air support were relayed up the ground chain of command and passed to the Flivo, and aircraft usually arrived overhead within two to three hours. In the panzer groups, the liaison officers were equipped with light armored vehicles and often accompanied the lead tank columns, particularly in those supporting Richthofen's Fliegerkorps VIII, the Luftwaffe's preeminent group support force. Flivo numbers were steadily expanded and by the beginning of the October offensive against Moscow, Fliegerkorps II had 31 Flivos assigned to the formations it was supporting. By 1942, Flivos began to be assigned to the regimental level. Heer units and Luftwaffe aircraft still had difficulties with radio communications, and swastika banner recognition flags on tanks and vehicles, smoke, and colored panels were used to identify German troops to friendly aircraft. Incidents of "friendly fire" were not uncommon, particularly when the panzer forces drove rapidly behind enemy lines.

Despite the close Luftwaffe–Heer staff coordination, the limited aircraft available led to tensions between army and air commanders during the campaign, as the Luftwaffe lacked the numbers needed to meet all the army's demands for air support and fighter cover as German forces drove deeper into the vast expanse of the USSR. Dogged resistance by the Red Army and VVS led to incessant calls from army commanders for Stukas for ground support and Bf 109s to cover the troops from the increasing numbers of Il-2 Shturmoviks. In response, Luftflotte 2 and 4 organized special close-combat leader (*Nahkampfführer*) task forces to improve close-air support operations on specific sectors of the front.

Tactics and aircraft

German fighter pilots dominated the skies over the USSR during the early years of the war on the Eastern Front. The Luftwaffe had developed "Rotte" and "Schwarm" tactics, based on their Spanish Civil War experience, that would ultimately be adopted by their Soviet, RAF, and USAAF opponents. In each two-ship Rotte, the leader engaged enemy aircraft while the wingman defended his tail. Two Rotte were grouped into "finger-four" Schwarm formations. The Rotte and Schwarm proved devastatingly superior to the less flexible three-plane Vics used by most air forces at the start of the war, including the VVS. Luftwaffe fighter pilots were experienced veterans, with hundreds of training and combat hours in their logbooks, and radios in every aircraft to coordinate their attacks. German fighter pilot culture focused on seeking out and shooting down the enemy in the air above all else, and Rotte and Schwarms were often allowed to prowl the front on free-hunt (*Freie Jagd*) missions. As the Germans did not typically rotate pilots from frontline to other duties, the veteran Luftwaffe pilots began to accumulate large kill totals, and over the course of the war 103 aces claimed over 100 kills.

The Messerschmitt Bf (*Bayerische Flugzeugwerke*) 109 fighter gave the veteran German fighter pilots a superior combat aircraft in 1941. The majority of Bf 109s in the force in June 1941 were F-2 or F-4 (Friedrich) models, along with smaller numbers of Es (Emils) still in service. The F-2 and F-4 could fly at 550 or 560kph (341–347mph), respectively, and the Emil 525kph (326mph), far faster than the large numbers of obsolescent Soviet I-153s and I-16s in the VVS at the beginning of the war. Soviet fighters were more maneuverable, but the veteran Luftwaffe pilots avoided dogfights and used the Bf 109's superior speed to engage or disengage at will, launching repeated boom-and-zoom diving attacks on their slower opponents. Bf 109s carried 20mm cannon and 7.92mm machine guns, giving the fighters hard-hitting and concentrated firepower. Luftflotte 1 and 4 both had two Bf 109-equipped JGs (*Jagdgeschwaderen*) assigned, and Kesselring's Luftflotte 2, supporting Army Group Center's initial main attack, controlled three JGs.

The two-engine, two-seat Bf 110 Zerstörer (*Destroyer*) had been designed to serve as a long-range offensive fighter that would defeat enemy fighters and clear the way for the bombers. The aircraft had a powerful armament, with two 20mm cannon and four MG 15 7.92mm MGs in the nose and

The Hs 123 was an obsolete ground-support biplane that received a new lease of life on the Eastern Front. Hardy and reliable, it proved able to maintain operations in the primitive conditions in the east and was very popular with the army units it supported. In the later years of the war, the Luftwaffe emulated Soviet practice and used a variety of biplanes, including the Hs 123, for night harassment bombing operations. (Nik Cornish at www.stavka.photos/)

a further rear-firing 7.92mm for the radio operator. The Bf 110 had difficulties engaging the more maneuverable single-engine RAF fighters in 1940, but nevertheless proved to be an extraordinarily versatile aircraft, and was used as in the long-range reconnaissance, night fighter, and ground-attack roles. The Bf 110 E could near a top speed of 500kph (310mph) at an altitude of 3,000m (10,000ft), and in addition to its heavy cannon and machine-gun armament, could carry a 1,200kg (2,645lb) payload, twice that of the slower Il-2 Shturmovik. During *Barbarossa*, Bf 110 D and E fighter-bomber versions were initially assigned to Luftflotte 2. Fliegerkorps II contained Fast Bomber Wing (*Schnellkampfgeschwader*) SKG 210 with 83 Bf 110s, and 78 were in Destroyer Wing (*Zerstörergeschwader*) ZG 26 operating as part of Richthofen's Fliegerkorps VIII.

The Ju 87 Stuka, short for *Sturzkampfflugzeug* (dive bomber), rapidly established itself as the symbol of Luftwaffe power in Hitler's early Blitzkrieg victories. The Stuka's dive-bombing tactics gave it enough accuracy to be able to destroy point targets including bridges, bunkers, headquarters, and communications sites. The Ju 87 B-1 had a top speed of 383kph (237mph) at 4,000m (13,123ft), but could reach speeds of 500–600kph (310–372mph) when diving on its target. The maximum bombload consisted of a 250kg (551lb) bomb carried under the belly and four 50kg (110lb) bombs on wing racks. In addition to the more common Ju 87 B model, in June 1941 the force included a number of Ju 87 Rs with increased range from drop tanks carried under each wing, but only able to carry a single 250kg (551lb) bomb under the belly. The heavy Ju 87 with its fixed undercarriage was slow and vulnerable to enemy fighters, but effective if the Luftwaffe could ensure air superiority or provide fighter escort. Apart from a small number of Stukas operating in the far north as part of Luftflotte 5, all of the Luftwaffe Ju 87s operating against the USSR in June 1941 were concentrated in Luftflotte 2 in support of Army Group Center. Stukas of StG 1 and StG 2 flew in Richthofen's Fliegerkorps VIII, and StG (*Sturzkampfgeschwader*) 77 in Loerzer's Fliegerkorps II.

The Luftwaffe included three types of medium bombers in its June 1941 order of battle. The main level bomber was the Heinkel He 111 H, the rough equivalent of the Soviet DB-3, with two engines, a five-man crew, and the ability to carry 2,000kg of bombs on 483km (300-mile) missions. Range could be extended up to 645km (400 miles), but with a drastically reduced bombload of 500kg (1,102lb). Speeds ranged from 398kph to 435kph (247–270 mph) in the H-6 version. The He 111 was protected by some armor and three to eight MG 15 7.92mm machine guns, and the crews were trained to fly in protective formations, but the bomber was vulnerable to ground fire and enemy fighter attack. When bombing from 4,000m (13,123ft) to avoid enemy antiaircraft fire, the He 111 had poor accuracy, leading to the Luftwaffe's focus on dive bombing. The Luftwaffe continued to operate numbers of obsolescent Dornier Do 17Zs in June 1941, although it was in the process of replacing them with Ju 88s. Known as the flying pencil due to its thin fuselage, the Do 17 was an early 1930s civilian mail plane adopted for military use. It could reach 410kph (254mph), but was not as sturdy as the He 111, and had a smaller bombload of 1,000kg (2,204lb). The

The Luftwaffe was forced to rely heavily on its limited force of Ju 52 transports during Operation *Barbarossa* for logistical support both of its forward airfields and to fly fuel to advancing panzer divisions. By 1942, Ju 52s were pressed into service resupplying German ground units cut off by Soviet counteroffensives. (Nik Cornish at www.stavka.photos/)

General Alfred Keller commanded Luftflotte 1 during Operation *Barbarossa*. A veteran bomber pilot and enthusiastic Nazi, he retired from active duty in 1943 to head the NKSF, the National Socialist Flying Corps, the paramilitary aviation organization of the party. Keller is shown in NKSF uniform. (Wiki Commons)

most modern Luftwaffe bomber was the Junkers Ju 88 A, a remarkably flexible design that could perform both level- and dive-bombing attacks. It also served as a reconnaissance aircraft and, later in the war, as a capable night fighter.

He 111s flew in Luftflotte 2 in Fliegerkorps II's KG 52, and in Luftflotte 4 in Fliegerkorps V's KG 55, and in Fliegerkorps IV's KG 27 and KG 4. All Do 17s flew in KG 2 and 3 in Luftflotte 2. Ju 88 As flew in all of the Luftflotten. As the Stukas were concentrated in Luftflotte 2, the other air fleets often had to use their medium bombers for costly low-level close-support missions, for which the aircraft were unsuited. Keller's Luftflotte 1 was unique in that its only strike aircraft were Ju 88s, as it lacked any other dive-bomber or medium-bomber units in its initial order of battle.

In 1941, the Luftwaffe had only a few units specifically dedicated to the close support of ground forces. Fliegerkorps VIII contained *Schlachtflieger* (SG)/LG 2, which included 38 Bf 109 E-7s used as fighter bombers and 22 Henschel Hs 123 biplanes. The Henschels were obsolete single-seaters, with a weak armament of two 7.92mm machine guns and a 450kg (992lb) bomb-carrying capacity. The biplane was rugged, however, and proved able to continue operations in the difficult conditions on the Eastern Front. The Hs 123 was popular with the troops and continued in service into 1944. The Bf 109 fighter bombers could deliver four 55kg (121lb) bombs on the wings or a 250kg (551lb) on the center line.

Aerial reconnaissance was another area in which the Luftwaffe had a decided edge over the Soviet air arm in the early years of the war. Long-range reconnaissance assets were kept under Luftwaffe control, but short-range reconnaissance aircraft were assigned to the Heer, typically controlled by armies and panzer groups, and sometimes individual panzer divisions. These units flew the obsolete Henschel Hs 125, a parasol-winged monoplane, and Focke-Wulf Fw 189 aircraft dubbed the "flying eye," due to its extensively glazed cockpit.

Logistics and training

The Luftwaffe had succeeded in previous campaigns by keeping up strong support for the panzers with a mobile logistics capability able to rapidly set up operations at captured enemy airbases or on improvised airstrips. Airfield companies were flown into captured or improvised airfields by Ju 52s, while Luftwaffe motorized supply companies accompanied the advancing panzer units to provide fuel and munitions. Operating from forward allowed the Luftwaffe to outfly its opponents with high sortie rates, often four to six per aircraft per day. The system was optimized to support short offensive campaigns, and there was little attention given to aircraft maintenance and repairs during an advance. As a result, aircraft with even minor technical issues were taken off-line to be repaired after the campaign, and aircraft needing major work would be sent back to Germany to be rebuilt.

The German spring campaign in the Balkans illustrated the challenges that distance and poor communications posed to the Luftwaffe's mobile basing strategy. Richthofen's Fliegerkorps VIII struggled to displace 240km (149 miles) from its bases in Bulgaria to Greece, hindered by the poor road network, and had to rely heavily on Ju 52s to transport fuel and ammunition forward. For the campaign against the USSR, Axis forces would need to advance over 900km (560 miles), relying on a primitive communications network for logistics support. The western USSR only contained 82,000km (50,000 miles) of railroad track, and the rails would need to be converted to the European gauge. Rather than the prewar reports of 250,000km (155,000 miles) of all-weather roads, the advancing German forces only found about 65,000km (40,000 miles). The Luftwaffe had to operate from captured Soviet airbases either deliberately wrecked or damaged by battle, or improvised airstrips, and the primitive dirt roads made it difficult for the supply columns to reach them. The lack of emphasis on forward maintenance capabilities led to large numbers of aircraft with light damage or needing minor repairs being taken off flight-ready status and crowding the Luftwaffe's bases. The Luftwaffe's force of Junkers Ju 52 transports helped fly fuel and ammunition to the forward bases and were also frequently called to supply fuel to the panzer group spearheads, but the force was too small to meet more than a fraction of requirements.

The Luftwaffe's pilots and aircrew were the most experienced and arguably best trained in the world in 1941. German training programs ensured 250 hours of flight time, about 100 of these in the aircraft the pilots would fly in combat, before personnel joined their operational units. Luftwaffe pilots, aircrew, and ground personnel were also experienced, the force having fought a series of rapid, successful campaigns over the previous two years. However, the training establishment was relatively modest in 1941, and with no real reserves the Luftwaffe routinely mobilized its training assets, in particular Ju 52 aircraft and aircrew, for short-term augmentation of the operational force when on campaign. In June 1941, the Ju 52 inventory had been reduced due to the loss of almost 100 aircraft, many drawn from training units, during the costly airborne invasion of Crete the month before. The Luftwaffe was already short of pilots in 1941 and would soon have to shorten its training program.

Leaders

Battle-tested officers led the Luftwaffe on the Eastern Front in 1941. Luftflotte 1's commander, Generaloberst Alfred Keller, was born in 1882 and served in the German air service before 1914. Keller led the 1st Bomber Wing during World War I, served in the army after the Armistice, and transferred to the Luftwaffe when its existence was revealed by Hitler. Keller personally led his squadrons into battle over Dunkirk in 1940 before leading Luftflotte 1 east to prepare for Operation *Barbarossa* in 1941. Keller's single Fliegerkorps was led by General der Flieger Helmuth Förster, a highly decorated pilot from World War I who commanded a Luftwaffe division during the Polish campaign and served as Chief of Staff for Luftflotte 5 in 1940.

Förster was assigned to take over Fliegerkorps I on short notice when its previous commander, General Ulrich Grauert, was shot down and killed over the English Channel on May 15. Keller also controlled a small contingent for maritime operations designated Air Command Baltic and led by Oberstleutnant Wolfgang von Wild, a naval cadet during World War I who fought with right-wing forces in Silesia and Berlin during the war's chaotic aftermath. After joining the Weimar Republic navy in 1923, he transferred to the Luftwaffe in the 1930s.

Generalfeldmarschall Albert Kesselring commanded the largest of the Luftwaffe formations in June 1941, Luftflotte 2, supporting Army Group Center on the initial primary axis of attack. Kesselring was born in 1892 and served during World War I as an artilleryman and staff officer. An able administrator, Kesselring transferred to the new Luftwaffe in the 1930s. He commanded Luftflotte 1 during the Polish campaign

Kesselring (right, with General Bruno Loerzer) led Luftflotte 2 until a large portion of the force was transferred to the Mediterranean to operate against Malta in 1941. Kesselring oversaw the Axis defensive campaign in Italy in 1943–45. This photo was taken near Kopys in Russia in August 1941. (Getty Images)

and then Luftflotte 2 during the campaign for France and the Battle of Britain in 1940. Luftflotte 2 was involved in Mediterranean operations before being shifted north for *Barbarossa*, as was Kesselring's Fliegerkorps VIII, led by Wolfram Freiherr von Richthofen. Convinced to join the air service in 1918 by cousins Manfred and Lothar, Richthofen scored eight victories before the Armistice. He became German's leading pioneer of close-air support techniques while serving with the Condor Legion during the Spanish Civil War and led Fliegerkorps VIII in 1939 and 1940. A dynamic and ruthless leader, Richthofen incessantly darted around the battlefield in his Fieseler Storch liaison plane, often visiting various subordinates and ground force headquarters daily to coordinate and spur operations. His Fliegerkorps had the majority of the Stukas on the Eastern Front in 1941, and his expertise in close-air support led the VIII to be nicknamed the Close Air Support Corps (*Nahkampffliegerkorps*). In contrast, Göring regarded Loerzer, the commander of Kesselring's Fliegerkorps II and a World War I flier with 44 victories, to be a lazy commander.

Generaloberst Alexander Loehr led Luftflotte 4, supporting Army Group South. A native of Croatia, Loehr flew in the Austro-Hungarian armed forces during World War I and was the commander of the Austrian Air Force during the 1938 Anschluss. He led Luftflotte 4 from then onwards. Generalleutnant Kurt Pflugbeil led Loehr's Fliegerkorps IV, initially stationed in Romania, and General der Flieger Robert Ritter von Greim commanded Fliegerkorps V in southern Poland. Both officers would serve extensively on the Eastern Front. Von Greim was regarded by Hitler as one of his true fighting generals and was called to the Führerbunker in Berlin in May 1945 to be promoted to Field Marshal and given command of the Luftwaffe, a post he only held for a few days before the final collapse of Nazi Germany.

Axis allies

Romania, Hungary, Finland, and Italy committed significant air forces to the 1941 campaign, along with smaller elements from other Axis allies. During the first years of the war, Nazi Germany pursued policies aimed at keeping its allied air forces technologically weak and militarily dependent, and most Axis aircraft were inferior to those of the Luftwaffe. Bucharest joined the *Barbarossa* assault on June 22, and the Romanian Air Force (ARR) organized 253 of its 672 aircraft into the GAL (Combat Air Grouping) for operations against the USSR. Romanian airmen flew a mixture of indigenously designed German aircraft, including Bf 109 Es along with a number of British aircraft purchased before the war, including Hurricane fighters. The GAL was subordinated to Pflugbeil's Fliegerkorps IV and after suffering extensive losses during the siege of Odessa it was withdrawn for rebuilding. Luftwaffe General der Flieger Wilhelm Speidel commanded a separate mixed force of German fighter interceptors and flak units stationed in Romania to defend the Ploesti oil fields and associated infrastructure.

Hungary joined the conflict with the USSR on June 27. The Hungarian Air Force, the Magyar Királyi Honvéd Légierő (MKHL), had well-trained pilots, but its force of over 500 aircraft was largely obsolescent due to Hitler's reluctance to provide Budapest with capable aircraft that might be used against Romania. Italy filled the gap, and the small force dedicated to the operation against the USSR after Hungary joined the war consisted of Fiat CR.32 and CR.42 fighters, and Ca.135s as well as some Ju 86 bombers. After 1,454 sorties and 56 losses, the Hungarian air element was withdrawn from operations in the USSR for reconstitution in late 1941.

Italy dispatched an air corps of four squadrons organized as the 22nd Gruppo Autonomo C.T. to support the Italian Expeditionary Corps in Russia (CSIR). The unit consisted of 51 MC.2000 fighters along with three Ca.311s and two SM.81s supported by 1,900 personnel and 300 motor vehicles. The fighters and bombers were accompanied by 32 Ca.311s and

A Finnish fighter in 1941. Germany's allies contributed almost 1,000 additional aircraft to Operation *Barbarossa*. The Nazi regime, however, was hesitant about supplying its allies with the most modern aircraft types available, leaving the allies with a mix of indigenous production, foreign purchases, and less-capable German aircraft models. (Nik Cornish at www.stavka.photos/)

one SM.81 for reconnaissance and 20 SM.81s transports. The unit operated on the southern portion of the front.

Finland was initially hesitant to attack on June 22, but joined in the war against the Soviet Union four days later after Soviet artillery barrages against Finnish positions and VVS raids on bases in Finland holding German aircraft. The Finnish Air Force had worked to modernize after the 1939–40 Winter War, and now contained five fighter, three bomber, and five independent squadrons. The force brought 238 aircraft to the campaign, although the mix of indigenously produced, Soviet, German, British, French, Italian, American, and Dutch aircraft was only at 50 percent readiness when it began operations.

Organization

The Luftwaffe's highest field formation was the Luftflotte (air army), the equivalent of a US numbered air force. Three Luftflotten supported the Axis assault, with one assigned to support each of the three attacking army groups, and elements of Luftflotte 5 in Norway were sent to support the Axis attack in the far north. A Luftflotte was a "mini-Luftwaffe" and contained the full spectrum of fighter, bomber, and support aircraft needed for major operations along with a variety of command and control and ground-support units. Göring had ensured that the Luftwaffe controlled Germany's antiaircraft (flak) resources, and Luftflotte 2 and 4 each contained a full flak corps, while the smaller Luftflotte 1 contained several separate flak regiments. The three Luftflotten controlled a combined total of five Fliegerkorps (air corps), along with a mixture of support aircraft. Each Fliegerkorps consisted of a variety of Geschwaderen (air wings) that controlled a single type of aircraft and consisted of either bombers (KG), fighters (JG), Bf 110 twin-engine fighters (ZG), or fighter bombers (SKG), ground-attack aircraft (LG), or dive bombers (StG). A full-strength Geschwader would contain three or four 30-plane Gruppen. In turn, the Gruppe consisted of three Staffeln (squadrons). Fighter Staffel contained three Schwarm, each of four fighters, with each Schwarm containing two Rotten with a pilot and wingman. Bomber Staffeln consisted of four three-plane Kettes.

Luftwaffe order of battle, June 22, 1941					
Aircraft type	1st LF	2nd LF	4th LF	5th LF	Total
Bombers	270	240	360	10	880
Dive bombers	–	250	–	30	280
Single-engine fighters	110	270	210	10	600
Twin-engine fighters	–	60	–	–	60
Ground attack	–	60	–	–	60
Liaison	20 (30)	30 (30)	30 (50)	–	80 (110)
Long-range recon	50 (40)	30 (40)	30 (50)	10	120 (130)
Short-range recon	(110)	(110)	(140)	(10)	(370)
Transport	30	60	60	–	150
Total	660	1,180	930	70	2,840 (610)

Numbers in parentheses are additional aircraft directly assigned to army support.

LUFTFLOTTE 1 (Generaloberst Alfred Keller)

Fliegerkorps I (General der Flieger Helmuth Förster)
4., 5./JG 53 "Pik As" – Bf 109 E
Stab., I., II., III./JG 54 – Bf 109 F
Stab., II., III./KG 1 "Hindenburg" – Ju 88 A
Stab., I., II., III./KG 76 – Ju 88 A
Stab., I., II., III./KG 77 – Ju 88 A

Fliegerführer Ostsee (Oberstleutnant Wolfgang von Wild)
K.Gr. 806 – Ju 88 A
1.(F)/125 – He 59
2., 3.(F)/125 – He 114 and Ar 95

LUFTFLOTTE 2 (Generalfeldmarschall Albert Kesselring)

Stab, I., III./JG 53 "Pik As" – Bf 109 E
Stab., 2(F)/122 – Ju 88 A, Bf 110, Bf 109 E
Westa 26 – Bf 110, Do 17 Z, He 111 H

Stab., II., III./StG 1 – Ju 87 B
Stab., I., III./StG 2 "Immelmann" – Ju 87 B, Ju 87 R, Bf 110

Fliegerkorps VIII (General der Flieger Wolfram Freiherr von Richthofen)
Stab., II., III./JG 27 – Bf 109 F
II./JG 52 – Bf 109 E, F
Stab., I., II./ZG 26 "Horst Wessel" – Bf 110
II., 10 (S)/LG 2 (Bf 109 E, Hs 123)
Stab., I., 8. 9./KG 2 "Holzhammer" – Do 17 Z
III./KG 3 "Blitz" – Do 17 Z

Fliegerkorps II (General de Flieger Bruno Loerzer)
Stab., I., II., III., IV./JG 51 – Bf 109 F
Stab., I., II./SKG 210 – Bf 110
Stab., I., II./KG 3 "Blitz" – Do 17 Z
Stab., I., II., III./KG 52 "Legion Condor" – He 111 H, He 111 P
Stab., I., II., III./StG 77 – Ju 87 B

LUFTFLOTTE 4 (Generaloberst Alexander Loehr)

Fliegerkorps V (General der Flieger Robert Ritter von Greim)
Stab., I., II., III./JG 3 – Bf 109 F
Stab., II., III./KG 51 "Edelweiss" – Ju 88 A
Stab., I., II., III./KG 54 "Totenkopf" – Ju 88 A
Stab., I., II., III./KG 55 "Greif" – He 111 H, Bf 110

Stab., I., II., III./KG 77 – Ju 88 A
Fliegerkorps IV (Generalleutnant Kurt Pflugbeil)
Stab., II., III./JG 77 – Bf 109 E, Bf 109 F
I.(J)/LG 2 – Bf 109 E
Stab., I., II., III./KG 27 "Boelcke" – He 111 H
Stab., II./KG 4 "General Weaver" – He 111 H

LUFTFLOTTE 5 (Generaloberst Hans-Juergen Stumpff) – in the Nordic Countries

240 aircraft in total. The portion dedicated to operations against the USSR were:

Fliegerführer Kirkenes (Oberst Andreas Nielsen)
5./KG (10 Ju 88)
IV.(St)/LG 1 (36 Ju 87)

I.(J)/JG 77 (10 Bf 109 E)
I.(Z)/JG 77 (7 Bf 110)
Stab./ZG 76 (6 Bf 110)
I.(H)/32 (7 Hs 126, 3 Do 17)
I./KueFlGr 406 (He 115 and Do 18)

DEFENDER'S CAPABILITIES

Stalin's airpower

Stalin knew a war with Nazi Germany was coming, but, assuming Hitler wished to avoid a two-front war, expected that it would begin no earlier than 1942. When the invasion struck, it caught the Red Army and Air Force in the midst of frenetic and incomplete modernization and force expansion programs. Like Mussolini's Italy, the USSR had modernized too early, producing some of the best aircraft in the world during the mid-1930s, including the four-engine TB-3 long-range bomber, twin-engine SB fast bomber, maneuverable biplanes, and the I-16, the first low-wing monoplane fighter with retractable landing gear. After initial successes fighting in the Spanish Civil War, however, Soviet aircraft were outclassed by the German Condor Legion's more modern Bf 109s, Ju 87s, and He 111s. The massive purges of the armed forces and the abject failure of Soviet airpower during the Winter War with Finland in 1939–40 followed. The ensuing crash effort to expand, rearm, and reorganize the VVS led to turmoil and confusion, and the force had major shortfalls in organization, equipment, training, logistics, and leadership in June 1941.

One of Polikarpov's I-16 Rata/Ishak fighters in flight. A revolutionary design when it first took to the air in the early 1930s, the I-16 had a monoplane design and retractable landing gear. The maneuverable aircraft was effective in the early phase of the Spanish Civil War, but already outclassed when the first Condor Legion Bf 109s took to the air for Franco. (Getty Images)

Command and control

Soviet airpower heavily outnumbered their opponents in June 1941, with 7,133 aircraft in the five special military districts on the border, plus 1,339 bombers controlled by Long-Range Aviation (DBA) and another 1,445 controlled by the Baltic and Black Sea fleets. Unlike the Luftwaffe, Soviet airpower was distributed between a number of independent organizations. The aviation divisions of the Soviet Air Force (VVS) were assigned to and controlled by front headquarters – the rough equivalent of army groups in German and Axis armies – or by their subordinate armies. Four-engine TB-3 and twin-engine DB-3 and DB-3F bombers were separately organized as Long-Range Aviation (DBA), controlled by the Ministry of Defense in peacetime and the VVS High Command in wartime. Air defense fighters were integrated with antiaircraft units, spotters, and searchlight assets

OPPOSITE SOVIET AVIATION ORGANIZATION, JUNE 1941

into Homeland Air Defense (PVO) forces in four PVO regions, with particularly strong forces including a fighter corps each assigned to the defense of Leningrad and Moscow. Naval aviation assets were separately organized and placed under the fleets and flotillas. Naval aviation forces used the same aircraft types as the VVS apart from small numbers of seaplanes, but were focused on operations with the fleet and protection of naval bases. Civil Aviation (GVF) controlled civilian aviation resources and were mobilized with the German attack to support military operations.

The Commander-in-Chief of the VVS was responsible for training, doctrine, and logistics, but the operational control of VVS divisions was fragmented at the operational and tactical levels. Military district/front commanders controlled assigned VVS IADs (fighter divisions) and BABs (bomber divisions), while each subordinate-combined arms ground army controlled one or two SADs (mixed aviation divisions) with an assortment of fighter, ground-attack, and bomber regiments for direct support. On the wartime fronts activated in the west on June 22 – the Northwestern, Western, Southwestern, and Southern – 14 of the 24 aviation divisions were directly subordinated to ground force armies, with only ten controlled by the various front headquarters. The VVS soon discovered that army commanders were reluctant to release their assigned air divisions, making it impossible to concentrate airpower over the battle zone. The early wartime divisional organization proved to be too large, and commanders had particular difficulties controlling the various four-to-five fighter, bomber, or ground-attack regiments usually found in the mixed aviation divisions. The prewar 60–64 plane regiments were themselves too large for effective operations and required three airfields for proper basing.

Aviation division subordination in the western USSR, June 22, 1941			
	Assigned to army control	Controlled at front level	Army control/total divisions
Baltic Special Military District /Northwestern Front	6 SAD (8 A) 7 SAD (11 A) 8 SAD (27 A)	4 SAD 57 IAD*	3/5
Western SMD/ Western Front	9 SAD (10 A) 10 SAD (4 A) 11 SAD (3 A)	12 BAD 13 BAD 43 IAD**	3/6
Kiev SMD/ Southwestern Front	14 SAD (5 A) 62 BAD (5 A) 15 SAD (6 A) 16 SAD (6 A) 63 SAD (26 A) 64 SAD (12 A)	17 BAD 19 BAD 36 IAD*** 44 IAD	6/10
Odessa SMD/ Southern Front	20 SAD (9 A) 21 SAD (9 A)	43 SAD	2/3
Total	14	10	14/24

SAD = Mixed Aviation Division
BAD = Bomber Aviation Division
IAD = Fighter Aviation Division
*57 IAD focused on defense of Vilnius
**43 IAD focused on defense of Minsk
***36 IAD focused on defense of Kiev

Soviet aviation organization, June, 1941

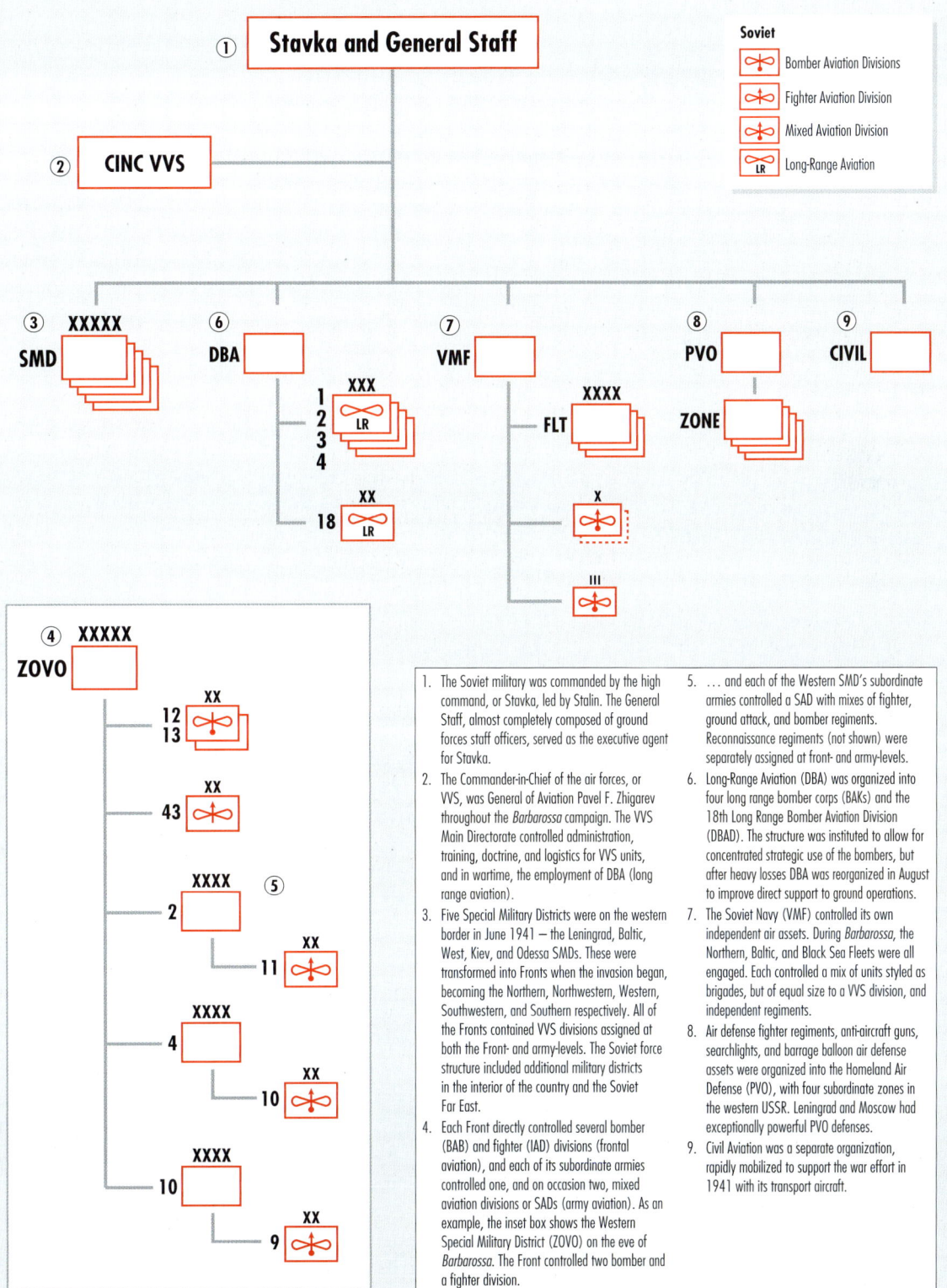

1. The Soviet military was commanded by the high command, or Stavka, led by Stalin. The General Staff, almost completely composed of ground forces staff officers, served as the executive agent for Stavka.

2. The Commander-in-Chief of the air forces, or VVS, was General of Aviation Pavel F. Zhigarev throughout the *Barbarossa* campaign. The VVS Main Directorate controlled administration, training, doctrine, and logistics for VVS units, and in wartime, the employment of DBA (long range aviation).

3. Five Special Military Districts were on the western border in June 1941 — the Leningrad, Baltic, West, Kiev, and Odessa SMDs. These were transformed into Fronts when the invasion began, becoming the Northern, Northwestern, Western, Southwestern, and Southern respectively. All of the Fronts contained VVS divisions assigned at both the Front- and army-levels. The Soviet force structure included additional military districts in the interior of the country and the Soviet Far East.

4. Each Front directly controlled several bomber (BAB) and fighter (IAD) divisions (frontal aviation), and each of its subordinate armies controlled one, and on occasion two, mixed aviation divisions or SADs (army aviation). As an example, the inset box shows the Western Special Military District (ZOVO) on the eve of *Barbarossa*. The Front controlled two bomber and a fighter division.

5. … and each of the Western SMD's subordinate armies controlled a SAD with mixes of fighter, ground attack, and bomber regiments. Reconnaissance regiments (not shown) were separately assigned at front- and army-levels.

6. Long-Range Aviation (DBA) was organized into four long range bomber corps (BAKs) and the 18th Long Range Bomber Aviation Division (DBAD). The structure was instituted to allow for concentrated strategic use of the bombers, but after heavy losses DBA was reorganized in August to improve direct support to ground operations.

7. The Soviet Navy (VMF) controlled its own independent air assets. During *Barbarossa*, the Northern, Baltic, and Black Sea Fleets were all engaged. Each controlled a mix of units styled as brigades, but of equal size to a VVS division, and independent regiments.

8. Air defense fighter regiments, anti-aircraft guns, searchlights, and barrage balloon air defense assets were organized into the Homeland Air Defense (PVO), with four subordinate zones in the western USSR. Leningrad and Moscow had exceptionally powerful PVO defenses.

9. Civil Aviation was a separate organization, rapidly mobilized to support the war effort in 1941 with its transport aircraft.

Aircraft

The VVS was in the process of reequipping with more modern aircraft, and in June 1941 its bases were packed with older models, many of them well used and requiring maintenance, along with increasing numbers of new production aircraft that few aircrews were trained to fly. Fully 75 percent of the fighter force were obsolete models, the majority of them I-16 fighters designed by Nikolai Polikarpov. The I-16 was a revolutionary design in 1933, with a monoplane configuration and retractable landing gear, and the USSR produced a total of 13,500. The stubby fighter was fast for its time with a top speed of 489kph (303mph) and highly maneuverable, but a tendency to spin made it a challenging machine for new pilots to master and earned it the nickname Ishak (Donkey). I-16s were initially successful in the Spanish Civil War and nicknamed Rata (Rat) by their Spanish and Condor Legion opponents, but they were outclassed when the Bf 109s arrived. In June 1941, the I-16s struggled to catch even Ju 88 bombers at 3,000m (9,842ft), the altitude where much of the air combat took place on the Eastern Front.

To replace the I-16, Polikarpov turned again to biplanes, and in 1939 the I-153 Chaika with a retractable undercarriage began to join the force. Perhaps the most capable biplane fighter ever produced, the Chaika was more maneuverable than the I-16, and Soviet air tacticians envisaged the I-153s dogfighting with enemy formations while the I-16s did repeated diving attacks. In the event, both I-16s and I-153s were outclassed by the speedy Bf 109s and their veteran Luftwaffe pilots, who themselves inflicted heavy losses on the Soviets with slashing attacks from above. The I-153's utility was further diminished by its weak armament of 7.62mm rifle-caliber machine guns that had difficulties downing German bombers even if they could be engaged. 1,100 I-153s were in the western USSR when the invasion began, some assigned to the ground-attack role. Ninety-nine I-15 and I-15bis fighters, a fixed undercarriage Polikarpov biplane design from the early 1930s, were still part of the force in 1941. The aircraft was maneuverable but cripplingly slow, poorly armed, and even more vulnerable to the Bf 109s than the I-16s and I-153s.

Polikarpov's I-153 Chaika (*Seagull*) was an excellent biplane design, but hopelessly outclassed when faced with veteran Luftwaffe pilots in their Bf 109s in 1941. Few I-153s survived the first months of Operation *Barbarossa*. (Getty Images)

Soviet bomber regiments in the western USSR were mostly equipped with the three-seat, twin-engine Tupolev SB high-speed bomber (*Skorostnoy Bombardirovshick*). When first introduced in the early 1930s, the lightly armored SBs with their 450kph (279mph) speed could outrun biplane fighters such as the 330kph (205mph) Heinkel He 51, but the high-speed monoplane fighters that entered service in the later part of the decade, in particular the Bf 109, eliminated the SB's advantage. The SB's four defensive 7.62mm machine guns proved ineffective in warding off attacks by the Bf 109s, and few of the 2,000 SBs in the western USSR survived the first few weeks of combat.

Most DBA bombers in June 1941, as well as for the rest of the conflict, were DB-3s or DB-3Fs (Il-4s). The DB-3 was similar in capability to the Heinkel He 111, with the DB-3 F featuring an improved airframe. Naval aviation operated the DB-3T torpedo bomber variant. Numbers of obsolete TB-3 four-engine bombers remained in the force and suffered heavy losses when used in the early weeks of the war. A modernized four-engine bomber, the TB-7 (Pe-8), had been in development since 1936, but due to difficulties in production only eight had joined the force by June 1941, and only half that number were operational. The TB-7s would prove unreliable when used against Berlin, and less than 100 were produced during the entire war.

The Red Air Force was in the midst of an effort to field modernized aircraft during June 1941, but even the new fighter designs were outmatched by the Bf 109 F. The MiG-3 had entered the force in the largest numbers by June 1941. The new fighter had a powerful, large Mikulin AM-35A V-12 engine that gave good performance at high altitudes, but the aircraft was heavy and lacked maneuverability at the medium and lower altitudes where most air combat took place on the Eastern Front. After 1941, production of the aircraft was halted in favor of other types, and factories working on its engines were switched to production of the similar AM-38 used in the Il-2 Shturmovik. The remaining MiG-3s were used after 1941 for high-altitude interception and reconnaissance missions. Only 322 of the new LaGG-3 fighter had been produced by June 1941, but it joined the VVS in large numbers

An SB bomber. Designed to outrun the biplane fighters of the 1930s, the SBs found themselves extremely vulnerable to enemy fighter attack in 1941. Initial command and control confusion led to SB units typically attacking without fighter escort, and in small, squadron-sized packets that did little to the enemy except allow Luftwaffe fighter pilots to increase their kill scores. (Nik Cornish at www.stavka.photos/)

later in 1941 and continued in service well into the war. The LaGG-3 was another mediocre design, and cynical pilots bitterly joked that "LaGG" was an abbreviation for the Russian phrase "guaranteed varnished coffin," as the airframe made heavy use of specially processed wood. The fighter would eventually be given a new radial engine after 1941, resulting in the improved La-5 and with the La-5FN, a fighter that was able to match German Bf 109 and Fw 190 fighters later in the war. The best of the new fighter designs, the Yak-1, was available in small but increasing numbers in 1941. The Yak-1 could match the Bf 109 Es if the pilots were equally capable, but it was outclassed by the speedier Fs. The early production Yak-1s also suffered from severe teething and quality control problems that were accentuated after *Barbarossa* as the Soviets evacuated military industries to the Urals. Upgraded to the Yak-3 and Yak-9 versions, the fighter would be the dominant design used by the VVS during the later years of the war.

New aircraft types produced at the beginning of Operation *Barbarossa*			
Type of aircraft	1940	Prior to June 22, 1941	Total
Yak-1	64	335	399
MiG-3	20	1,289	1,309
LaGG-3	–	322	322
PE-2	2	458	460
IL-2	–	249	249
Total	86	2,653	2,739

While the new generation of Soviet fighters had their flaws, the new light bomber and ground-attack aircraft joining the force in 1941 were exceptional designs. The Petlyakov Pe-2 was designed as a twin-engine fighter, but like the Bf 110 proved capable in a wide variety of roles, including dive bombing, level bombing, reconnaissance, and night fighting. The Il-2 Shturmovik ground-attack aircraft, the most famous Soviet aircraft of the war, was a unique design. With its pilot and engine heavily armored, the Il-2 was intended to survive in repeated low-level bombing, strafing, and rocket runs against enemy troops. The Shturmovik's impact in 1941 was limited by the small number available, with only a handful in frontline units in June, and by the difficulties of developing successful tactics during the disastrous months of 1941. Although the Shturmovik's armor was effective at protecting the aircraft from ground fire, German Bf 109 pilots soon learned to down Il-2s by attacking from the rear. The Shturmovik's effectiveness would dramatically improve in 1942 with increased numbers, more effective tactics, and the addition of a rear gunner position.

Training, logistics, and maintenance

Soviet problems with aircraft modernization were aggravated by training, maintenance, and personnel shortfalls. The VVS was not only attempting to absorb new aircraft, but it was engaged in a large-scale force expansion effort. Moscow planned to add 104 new regiments to the VVS and increase the aircraft inventory to 22,000. Only 19 of the new regiments were fully organized by June 1941, and others remained on paper or were only partially formed and lacked key officers, support personnel, and equipment. Force-wide maintenance and readiness rates were poor, with many of the older aircraft at the end of their service lives and a lack of spare parts and trained ground crew for the new models. Although 1,448 new-production aircraft had reached the frontline units, only 208 crews were fully qualified to fly the new models.

Stalin's invasion and seizure of Polish territory in 1939 saddled the VVS with the need to build a large number of new bases forward of its established prewar airfield network. Some

The mainstay of the DBA bomber force throughout the war was the DB-3/DB-3 F medium bomber. The DBA suffered heavy losses in bombing operations in 1941, and by 1942 was conducting operations almost completely at night. (Getty Images)

of the bases near the border were adequately equipped but overcrowded, while those to the immediate rear were much less developed, making it difficult for the forward units to disperse to rearward bases if attacked. Most Soviet airfields lacked antiaircraft capabilities and adequate dispersal areas. The aircraft were uncamouflaged due to orders from Stalin, who remained concerned that such actions could provoke the German attack he was determined to delay.

The VVS had a large but inefficient training establishment, and with the 1940 plans for VVS expansion, the high command ordered flight training accelerated in March. Additional directives in December and February 1941 further shortened training programs. Graduates of flying schools often arrived at their new units without the minimum required 35–55 flying hours in their logbooks, and what training they had was on obsolete aircraft. Once they reached their operational regiments, the pilots had little hope of additional training due to the pressures of the modernization program, along with commanders' fears that any training accidents would be considered potential sabotage and draw the attention of the NKVD. During the first three months of 1941, PVO pilots flew an average total of 15.5 hours, Western Special Military District pilots nine, and Kiev Special Military District pilots only four. The need to train on the new production aircraft was also a challenge. The Western Special Military District had 201 MiG-3s and 37 MiG-1s on June 22, but only 64 pilots were trained to fly them in good weather conditions, and four fully qualified for night and all-weather operations. Even Soviet veterans of Spain or Finland were at a severe disadvantage when facing the Luftwaffe, as most VVS aircraft were only equipped with radio receivers and not transmitters, and the fighters were still trained to fly in vulnerable three-ship Vics. The three-plane formation was awkward and difficult to maneuver, and the pilots spent more time concentrating on maintaining their formation and looking at the other two planes than scanning for enemy aircraft.

OPPOSITE INITIAL DISPOSITION OF LUFTWAFFE AND SOVIET AVIATION FORCES, JUNE 22, 1941

Leadership

Stalin's purge of the military began in 1937 and devastated the leadership of the VVS as well as the other armed services. Of the VVS's cadre of 13,000 officers, 4,724 were arrested, imprisoned, executed, or expelled from the service. The commander of the VVS, Yakov I. Alkanis, was arrested in the first wave of the repression in 1937 and executed in 1938. While numbers of purged Red Army ground force officers were later rehabilitated and returned to service, in the air forces only 892 of the 5,616 officers purged by 1940 returned during the war. Aircraft design institutes and factories were not immune, with thousands arrested for suspected sabotage. Aircraft designer K.A. Kalinin was among those arrested and executed, while Andrei Tupolev and others were sent to work in special NKVD prisons for designers. Political commissars now supervised commanders at all levels, and training and operations tempo decreased as even minor accidents could be reported and investigated by the NKVD as potential sabotage. The purges created a climate of fear and caution in the ranks of the leadership, with commanders reluctant to take initiative and conditioned to wait for and follow, to the letter, orders received from above. The removal of large numbers of commanders led to the shortening of officer training by one third, and the rapid promotion of inexperienced leaders to fill the gaps in leadership positions. By June 1941, 91 percent of the commanders at all levels in the Air Force had been in their positions for less than six months.

Yakov Smushkevich served as commander of the VVS from 1939 to 1940, and afterwards as Inspector-General of the Air Force. Despite his vigorous efforts to improve training, Smushkevich was swept up by the NKVD with other senior Air Force leaders in a new wave of purges, and after torture he was executed with many of his compatriots in late October. Smushkevich was rehabilitated after Stalin's death in 1953, and his awards posthumously reinstated in 1957. (Wiki Commons)

The huge VVS losses in the early days of *Barbarossa* drew renewed NKVD attention. Of the four VVS commanders of the Special Military Districts in the western USSR on June 22, one committed suicide and two were arrested within days of the German assault. All of the VVS's last three prewar commanders, A. Loktionov, Yakov V. Smushkevich, and P.V. Rychagov, were arrested and executed. Yakov V. Smushkevich, twice made a Hero of the Soviet Union for his service in Spain and during the Khalkhin-Gol battle with the Japanese, had served as VVS commander in 1939 at the age of 37, and ten months later was appointed Inspector General of the Air Force. His successor, P.V. Rychagov, was only 29 when he became the Air Force commander and had been a lieutenant three years before. Rychagov was relieved shortly before *Barbarossa* due to the VVS's accident rate and with Smushkevich was executed in October with a number of other VVS officers. General Pavel Zhigarev was promoted at the age of 41 to command of the Air Force just before the *Barbarossa* attack, largely due to the lack of other surviving senior staff, and despite the defeats of June remained in the position until replaced in early 1942 by Alexander Novikov. Zhigarev survived and was transferred to command VVS forces in the Far East.

SOVIET ORDER OF BATTLE

VVS Leningrad Military District/VVS Northern Front:
General A.A. Novikov
1st Mixed Aviation Division – subordinate to 14th Army, Murmansk–Kandalaksha area
10th Bomber Aviation Regiment
137th Bomber Aviation Regiment
145th Fighter Aviation Regiment
147th Fighter Aviation Regiment

55th Mixed Aviation Division – subordinate to 7th Army, north of Leningrad
72nd Fast Bomber Aviation Regiment

5th Mixed Aviation Division – subordinate to 23rd Army, Karelian Isthmus
7th Fighter Aviation Regiment
159th Fighter Aviation Regiment
158th Fighter Aviation Regiment

41st Bomber Aviation Division – subordinate to 23rd Army, Siverskaya area
201st Fast Bomber Aviation Regiment
202nd Fast Bomber Aviation Regiment
205th Fast Bomber Aviation Regiment

3rd Fighter Aviation Division – assigned to the defense of Leningrad
19th Fighter Aviation Regiment
44th Fighter Aviation Regiment

54th Fighter Aviation Division – assigned to the defense of Leningrad
26th Fighter Aviation Regiment
157th Fighter Aviation Regiment
311th Reconnaissance Aviation Regiment

2nd Mixed Aviation Division – south of Leningrad
2nd Fast Bomber Aviation Regiment
44th Fast Bomber Aviation Regiment
58th Fast Bomber Aviation Regiment
65th Fast Bomber Aviation Regiment

39th Fighter Aviation Division, south of Leningrad
154th Fighter Aviation Regiment
155th Fighter Aviation Regiment
156th Fighter Aviation Regiment

Total: 1,270 aircraft

VVS Baltic Special Military District/VVS Northwestern Front
312th Reconnaissance Aviation Regiment
4th Mixed Air Division
38th Fighter Aviation Regiment
35th Fast Bomber Aviation Regiment
50th Fast Bomber Aviation Regiment
53rd Fast Bomber Aviation Regiment

6th Mixed Air Division – subordinate to 8th Army
21st Fighter Aviation Regiment
31st Fast Bomber Aviation Regiment
40th Bomber Aviation Regiment
148th Fighter Aviation Regiment

7th Mixed Air Division – subordinate to 11th Army
10th Fighter Aviation Regiment
9th Fast Bomber Aviation Regiment
46th Bomber Aviation Regiment
241st Fast Bomber Aviation Regiment

8th Mixed Aviation Division – subordinate to 27th Army
15th Fighter Aviation Regiment
31st Fighter Aviation Regiment
61st Ground Attack Aviation Regiment

57th Fighter Aviation Division
42nd Fighter Aviation Regiment
54th Fast Bomber Aviation Regiment
49th Fighter Aviation Regiment

Total: 1,211 aircraft

VVS Western Special Military District/VVS Western Front
313th, 314th Reconnaissance Air Regiment
9th Mixed Air Division – subordinate to 10th Army
13th Fast Bomber Aviation Regiment
41st Fighter Aviation Regiment
124th Fighter Aviation Regiment
126th Fighter Aviation Regiment
129th Fighter Aviation Regiment

10th Mixed Air Division – subordinate to 4th Army
33rd Fighter Aviation Regiment
74th Ground Assault Aviation Regiment
123rd Fighter Aviation Regiment
39th Fast Bomber Aviation Regiment

11th Mixed Air Division – subordinate to 3rd Army
16th Fast Bomber Aviation Regiment
122nd Fighter Aviation Division
127th Fighter Aviation Division

12th Bomber Aviation Division
6th Fast Bomber Aviation Regiment
43rd Fast Bomber Aviation Regiment
128th Fast Bomber Aviation Regiment
209th Fast Bomber Aviation Regiment
215th Fast Bomber Aviation Regiment

13th Bomber Aviation Division
24th Fast Bomber Aviation Regiment
97th Fast Bomber Aviation Regiment
121st Fast Bomber Aviation Regiment
125th Fast Bomber Aviation Regiment
130th Fast Bomber Aviation Regiment

43rd Fighter Aviation Division
160th Fighter Aviation Regiment
161st Fighter Aviation Regiment
162nd Fighter Aviation Regiment
163rd Fighter Aviation Regiment

Total: 1,789 aircraft (252 modern fighter types)

VVS Kiev Special Military District/VVS Southwestern Front
315th and 316th Reconnaissance Air Regiment
14th Mixed Air Division – subordinate to 5th Army
17th Fighter Aviation Regiment
46th Fighter Aviation Regiment
89th Fighter Aviation Regiment

62nd Bomber Aviation Division – subordinate to 5th Army
52nd Fast Bomber Aviation Regiment
94th Fast Bomber Aviation Regiment
243rd Fast Bomber Aviation Regiment
245th Fast Bomber Aviation Regiment

15th Mixed Air Division – subordinate to 6th Army
23rd Fighter Aviation Regiment
28th Fighter Aviation Regiment
66th Ground Attack Regiment
164th Fighter Aviation Regiment

16th Mixed Air Division – subordinate to 6th Army
86th Fast Bomber Aviation Regiment
87th Fighter Aviation Regiment
92nd Fighter Aviation Regiment
226th Fast Bomber Aviation Regiment
227th Fast Bomber Aviation Regiment

63rd Mixed Air Division – subordinate to 26th Army
20th Fighter Aviation Regiment
62nd Ground Attack Aviation Regiment
91st Fighter Aviation Regiment
165th Fighter Aviation Regiment

64th Mixed Air Division – subordinate to 12th Army
12th Fighter Aviation Regiment
149th Fighter Aviation Regiment
166th Fighter Aviation Regiment
246th Fighter Aviation Regiment
247th Fighter Aviation Regiment

17th Bomber Aviation Division
48th Fast Bomber Aviation Regiment
224th Fast Bomber Aviation Regiment
225th Fast Bomber Aviation Regiment
242nd Fast Bomber Aviation Regiment

36th Fighter Aviation Division (Kiev area)
2nd Fighter Aviation Regiment
43rd Fighter Aviation Regiment
254th Fighter Aviation Regiment
255th Fighter Aviation Regiment

19th Bomber Aviation Division
33rd Fast Bomber Aviation Regiment
136th Bomber Aviation Regiment
138th Fast Bomber Aviation Regiment

44th Fighter Aviation Division (Vinnitsa area)
88th Fighter Aviation Regiment
248th Fighter Aviation Regiment
249th Fighter Aviation Regiment
252nd Fighter Aviation Regiment

Total: 1,913 aircraft

VVS Odessa Military District/VVS Southern Front
20th Mixed Air Division
4th Fighter Aviation Regiment
45th Fast Bomber Aviation Regiment
55th Fighter Aviation Regiment
211th Fast Bomber Aviation Regiment

21st Mixed Air Division
5th Bomber Aviation Regiment
69th Fighter Aviation Regiment
67th Fighter Aviation Regiment
168th Fighter Aviation Regiment
229th Fast Bomber Aviation Regiment

45th Mixed Air Division
131st Fighter Aviation Regiment
132nd Fast Bomber Aviation Regiment
232nd Fast Bomber Aviation Regiment
210th Fast Bomber Aviation Regiment

Total: 930 aircraft (including over 100 MiG-3 fighters)

Long-Range Bomber Aviation (DBA)
1st Long Range Bomber Aviation Corps
40th Long Range Bomber Aviation Division
53rd Long Range Bomber Aviation Regiment
200th Long Range Bomber Aviation Regiment
7th TBDAP
51st Long Range Bomber Aviation Division
7th Long Range Bomber Aviation Regiment
203rd Long Range Bomber Aviation Regiment
204th Long Range Bomber Aviation Regiment

2nd Long Range Bomber Aviation Corps
35th Long Range Bomber Aviation Division
100th Long Range Bomber Aviation Regiment
219th Long Range Bomber Aviation Regiment
223rd Long Range Bomber Aviation Regiment

48th Long Range Bomber Aviation Division
51st Long Range Bomber Aviation Regiment
220th Long Range Bomber Aviation Regiment
221st Long Range Bomber Aviation Regiment
222nd Long Range Bomber Aviation Regiment

3rd Long Range Bomber Aviation Corps
52nd Long Range Bomber Aviation Division
3rd TBDAP
98th Long Range Bomber Aviation Regiment
212th Long Range Bomber Aviation Regiment

42nd Long Range Bomber Aviation Division
1st TBDAP
96th Long Range Bomber Aviation Regiment
207th Long Range Bomber Aviation Regiment

4th Long Range Bomber Aviation Corps
22nd Long Range Bomber Aviation Division
8th Long Range Bomber Aviation Regiment
11th Long Range Bomber Aviation Regiment
21st Long Range Bomber Aviation Regiment

50th Long Range Bomber Aviation Division
81st Long Range Bomber Aviation Regiment
299th Long Range Bomber Aviation Regiment
231st Long Range Bomber Aviation Regiment
228th Long Range Bomber Aviation Regiment

18th Long Range Bomber Aviation Division (Independent)
14th TBDAP
90th Long Range Bomber Aviation Regiment
93rd Long Range Bomber Aviation Regiment

In total 1,332 aircraft, including 1,122 DB-3s and DB-3Ts, 201 TB-3s, and nine TB-7s

VVS SF (Northern Fleet) General
72nd Mixed Aviation Regiment
118th Reconnaissance Aviation Regiment
49th Reconnaissance Aviation Squadron

Total: 116 aircraft

VVS KBF (Red Banner Baltic Fleet) General-Mayor Mikhail Samokhin
8th Bomber Aviation Brigade
10th Bomber Aviation Brigade
61st Fighter Aviation Brigade
15th Reconnaissance Aviation Regiment
7 additional independent aviation Eskadrilas

Total 707 aircraft

VVS ChF (Black Sea Fleet)
62nd Fighter Aviation Brigade
63rd Bomber Aviation Brigade
119th Reconnaissance Aviation Regiment
11 additional independent aviation Eskahdrilas

Total of 624 aircraft
Northern, Red Banner Baltic, and Black Sea Fleets total 1,443 aircraft, 763 fighters (72 MiG-3s, 344 I-16s, rest I-153s and I-15bis), 217 bombers, 120 mine-torpedo aircraft (DB-3 and DB-3F), and 345 reconnaissance flying boats

An LaGG-3 in 1943. The LaGG-3 was heavy and underpowered, but over 6,000 were produced and it served throughout the first years of the war. The design was dramatically improved when a new radial engine was fitted into the La-5, and the later La-5FN and La-7 proved to be some of the most capable Soviet fighter designs of the war. (Wiki Commons)

CAMPAIGN OBJECTIVES

Conquest in the east

With the invasion across the English Channel postponed, Hitler determined to strike the USSR, expecting to destroy the Soviet regime in a rapid campaign and thereby, according to his convoluted reasoning, convincing Britain that it had no option but to leave the war. Operation *Barbarossa* was intended to accomplish Hitler's longstanding geostrategic goals of eliminating what he considered the "Judeo-Bolshevik" threat to Europe and seizing the resources and *Lebensraum* (living space) needed for his thousand-year Reich. The Nazi leadership considered the war to be an existential clash of ideologies, entailing the extermination and subjugation of whole populations. Militarily, the victories of 1939 and 1940 produced an attitude of supreme confidence in the German high command, and Chief of the Luftwaffe General Staff Jeschonnek exclaimed that Germany would at last have "a proper war" when he learned of the *Barbarossa* plan. Hitler and his planners assumed victory over the USSR could be obtained in a matter of weeks or, at the most, months. German Luftwaffe-supported panzer and infantry forces would rapidly encircle and destroy the Soviet army on the border and expected only fragmentary resistance thereafter. Panzer-led drives would follow to seize Leningrad, Kiev, the Donbas, and ultimately, Moscow. German forces were to establish a security line stretching from Arkhangelsk to Astrakhan, the "A–A" line, from which the Luftwaffe could, if necessary, launch long-range bombing raids to destroy any surviving Soviet war industries in the Ural Mountains.

Although Luftwaffe commanders also expected only a relatively brief campaign, its planners realized operations in the Soviet Union would be unlike those in the first two years of the war. The fronts in the USSR would be so large that airpower would be unable to concentrate on a single axis of attack. In the west, the Luftwaffe was able to operate one aircraft above every 20 square miles of the battlefield; in the western USSR, the ratio would be one for every 95. The Luftwaffe would have to support the three major ground force assaults aimed at Leningrad, Moscow, and the Ukraine, and the ground and air forces would increasingly diverge as they drove further east. The Luftwaffe was only able to allocate roughly

60 percent of its resources for *Barbarossa*, as Hitler ordered that it simultaneously continue operations against Britain, in the Mediterranean, and against the North Atlantic sea lanes. Heavily committed in three major theaters, the Luftwaffe would have no major reserves available if *Barbarossa* did not prove as rapid a success as expected.

Unlike during the lead-up to the Polish and French campaigns, the Luftwaffe did not have an interlude for rest and reconstitution before *Barbarossa* as operations continued throughout 1940–41 against Britain, in the Balkans and the Middle East. The Luftwaffe's preeminent close-support organization, General der Flieger Wolfram von Richthofen's Fliegerkorps VIII, had been heavily engaged during the Battle of Britain in 1940, when it had to withdraw its Ju 87 Stukas due to losses to RAF fighters, and in the Balkans in 1941. Richthofen's airmen were still engaged with the Royal Navy around Crete in May when he was called to Potsdam to begin arranging for the transfer of his forces to northern Poland for *Barbarossa*.

Hitler's *Barbarossa* Directive tasked the Luftwaffe with defending Germany against any Soviet air attack, providing adequate support to the offensive to destroy the enemy air force, supporting the army's advance, interdicting Soviet lines of communications, and conducting parachute operations if needed. OKL Chief of Staff Jeschonnek and his operations chief General Hoffmann von Waldau outlined the general guidance for the operation, and Luftflotte and Fliegerkorps staffs conducted the refined planning for the initial stages of *Barbarossa*. At a series of joint air–ground force planning conferences, the Luftwaffe resisted the army's desire for air support to attack divisions from the first day, insisting it first gain air superiority by attacking the enemy's airfields.

Luftwaffe planners assigned the largest force, Kesselring's Luftflotte 2, to support Army Group Center's main effort against Minsk and Smolensk, while Generaloberst Keller's much smaller Luftflotte 1 supported Army Group North's attack through the Baltic States towards Leningrad. Loehr's Luftflotte 4 was assigned to assist Army Group South as it attacked towards Kiev and the Donbas. A small maritime unit was attached to Luftflotte 1 for operations over the Baltic Sea, while to the south Luftflotte 4's Fliegerkorps IV was assigned operations over the Black Sea as a secondary mission. Uncertainties remained with both the Heer and the Luftwaffe about the priority and sequence of objectives after the expected destruction of the Red Army in the border region, with many generals favoring Moscow as the key objective, while Hitler rated objectives on the flanks – Leningrad, Crimea, Donbas, and ultimately the oilfields of the Caucasus – as higher priorities. The Führer was always sensitive to potential enemy threats to Ploesti in Romania and considered the Crimea to be an unsinkable aircraft carrier able to base long-range Soviet bombers for attacks on its oilfields and refineries.

Pavel Zhigarev served as VVS Commander-in-Chief throughout Operation *Barbarossa* and unlike his three predecessors, he was not executed for the poor performance of Soviet airpower in 1941. Under his leadership, the VVS headquarters improved its ability to support the force logistically, and with better tactical guidance. Zhigarev was transferred to the Far East in early 1942 and replaced by the capable Alexander Novikov. Zhigarev again commanded the Air Force from 1949 to 1957 and is pictured here postwar. (Wiki Commons)

Mussolini, Göring, and Hitler pictured at the Russian front in October 1941. Göring was initially hesitant about the invasion of the USSR, and only occasionally interceded in Luftwaffe operations in the east in 1941. In contrast, Operation *Barbarossa* saw Hitler take increasing control over military operations, directing forces towards Leningrad and Kiev in August against the protests of many of his senior generals and issuing his first "stand fast" order to German forces during the winter. (Getty Images)

Luftflotte 1 and 2 staffs war-gamed the *Barbarossa* plan and discussed potential operations with their key army counterparts, the panzer group commanders, but Loehr was diverted by the campaign in the Balkans and could only send a small liaison element to participate. Despite the pervasive optimism about German capabilities, there was a realization of the challenges that the Luftwaffe would face during the summer campaign, and on February 27, Luftwaffe Chief of Staff General Hans Jeschonnek noted to the OKH Chief General Franz Halder that operating on such a vast front would mean that the Luftwaffe would lack the numbers to maintain air superiority everywhere. German air assets would need to be concentrated on key sectors, and ground forces would have to prepare themselves for potential Soviet air attack in areas the Luftwaffe would be unable to cover.

In Moscow, Stalin clung to the hope that his 1939 non-aggression pact with Hitler would buy additional time for the modernization and reorganization of the Red Army and Air Force, the shortcomings of which had been exposed during the 1939–40 Winter War with Finland. Despite evidence of the Wehrmacht's preparations in the spring of 1941 for *Barbarossa*, the Soviet dictator forbade camouflage or dispersal at airfields in the border military districts, as he felt such measures could serve as a provocation for a German attack, potentially one launched not by the Führer but by some of his generals. As the full scope of the offensive and the extent of Soviet losses became evident in late June, it became clear to Stalin that the Soviet state was engaged in an existential struggle for survival.

Stalin had driven the prewar planning assessment that any major German attack would primarily focus on the Ukraine, and the Kiev Special Military District under General Mikhail Kirponos, one of the more competent officers to survive the purges, had been heavily reinforced. His air component was also the largest in the western USSR, controlling ten of the 24 aviation divisions in the four Special Military Districts on the frontier. As the German attack began, Stalin and his high command ordered that the prewar plans for immediate counterattacks – first to drive the enemy back to the frontier, and subsequently to strike into enemy territory – be executed. The orders were impossible to carry out due to the limited capabilities of Soviet ground and air forces at the time, and the huge losses already suffered from the surprise *Barbarossa* attack.

THE CAMPAIGN

Spearheading the invasion

June 22, 1941

The first airstrike of Operation *Barbarossa* was delivered by Bf 110s of ZG 26, "Horst Wessel," one of Richthofen's Fliegerkorps VIII units, against the Soviet Baltic Special Military District's 15 IAP (Fighter Aviation Regiment) at Alytus airfield. The Bf 110s proved extremely useful during the campaign, particularly in strikes against Soviet troops and line-of-communication targets. (Getty Images)

Luftwaffe planners were concerned with the timing of *Barbarossa*'s opening artillery barrage just before dawn as they lacked bomber crews trained in night formation flying. To prevent the Soviets from getting fighters aloft before the first strikes arrived, 30 select night-capable bomber crews flying He 111s, Ju 88s, and Do 17s were sent to attack ten Soviet airfields to disrupt any response before the following massed raids reached their targets. The first pilots and crews to cross the border in the early morning hours noted with surprise the lack of any reaction below. Hauptmann Johannes Freiherr von Richthofen's ZG 26 Bf 110s made faster time on their approach flight than expected, giving the VVS fighters at Alytus airfield the distinction of being the first Soviet airfield to be attacked just before 0400hrs. The Zerstörers rapidly destroyed 40 of the 62 new MiG-3 fighters parked in neat rows on the base. The scene was repeated many times that morning, as the first wave's 637 bombers and Stukas and 231 fighters bombed and strafed over 30 Soviet airfields from the Baltic to the Black Sea, followed by a second wave of 400 bombers covered by additional Bf 109s. The Luftwaffe's SD-2 "Butterfly" canister bombs, each delivering 96 submunitions, were particularly effective against the parked aircraft, and any unexploded bomblets created instant minefields on the airstrips. The weather was excellent with few clouds, and as they would do on many days during the summer, the German airmen were each able to fly multiple sorties. Bombers flew as many as six and the Bf 109s and Stukas as many as eight sorties.

Soviet commanders and personnel were stunned by the initial strikes. Stalin had at last been persuaded after midnight to issue orders for the military districts to improve their readiness, although he still expected limited provocations from a portion of the German force rather than a full invasion. Some units in the Kiev and Odessa Special Military Districts were able to take preparatory measures, but the order reached few VVS airfields in the Baltic and Western Special Military Districts before the attack. At Ternopil, Lieutenant aron Shapiro of the 86 ShAP (Ground Attack Regiment), like US personnel at Pearl Harbor six months later, initially thought the three bombers approaching the base were part of a readiness test. As the KG 51 Ju 88s began their attacks, airfield personnel could only reply with small arms fire as, like most VVS airfields, Ternopil lacked effective antiaircraft defenses. Nine SBs and two Pe-2s of the regiment's 64 aircraft were destroyed in the first raid.

The Western Special Military District's 10 Mixed Aviation Division (SAD) suffered some of the heaviest losses. Bombers from KG 3 struck the division's 39 SBAP (High-Speed Bomber Regiment) at its Pinsk airfield, destroying 43 SB bombers and five new Pe-2s on the ground. At the airfield at Brest, JG 51 Bf 109s destroyed 20 fighters of the 33 IAP in its first raid. A second attack by nine more Bf 109s strafed the airfield for another 40 minutes and reported the destruction of an additional 21 I-16s and five I-153s. Fifty aircraft were lost to SKG 210 Bf 110s at the 10 SAD's divisional headquarters airfield at Kobrin.

Some VVS fighters taxied around burning wrecks to take off, although most frontline leaders were paralyzed by the confusing orders from Moscow, which still limited Soviet actions, and fear of NKVD reprisals for any measures taken without full authorization. Probably the first air-to-air engagement took place when nine I-153 Chaika biplane fighters from Major Boris Surin's 123 IAP of the 10 SAD took off from Kobrin and shot down a StG 77 Stuka heading to attack the Brest Fortress. Veteran Bf 109 pilots of JG 51 intercepted the Chaikas and claimed several kills in return, likely the first Luftwaffe aerial victories of the air war in the east, with Lieutenant Franz Hahn of JG 51 shooting down three Soviet aircraft.

Panicked reports of attacks from the forward airfields were at first met with disbelief, and Stalin initially clung to his hope they were local attacks by German generals rather than a full-scale invasion. Defense Commissar Timoshenko informed the Western Military District in the early morning hours that Stalin still forbade any use of artillery against German forces. By 0715hrs, however, it was clear that a major offensive was underway, and Stalin authorized Soviet forces to attack any invaders that had violated the border, although ground troops were not to cross into enemy territory without special instructions. The VVS was given wildly unrealistic orders to identify concentrations of enemy air and ground forces and destroy the Luftwaffe at its bases "with powerful strikes by bomber and ground attack aviation." Enemy ground force groupings were to be bombed up to 100km to 150km (62–93 miles) into enemy territory, and Königsberg destroyed from the air. On the evening of the first day, new orders were issued to the Red Army to carry the war into enemy territory, but Moscow was hopelessly out of touch with the confusion and huge losses already caused by the initial German air and ground assaults.

By mid-morning, the Western Military District's bomber divisions were sent to strike the advancing German columns. With the VVS command and control system in a state of chaos, bomber squadrons were dispatched when ready to fly, and usually arrived over their targets

The opening blow (overleaf)

Bf 110s of ZG 26 led by Hauptmann Johannes Freiherr von Richthofen launched the first attack of Operation *Barbarossa* around 0315hrs on June 22, arriving over Alytus airfield a few minutes before the other Luftwaffe attack aircraft. The Messerschmitt's yellow fuselage markings appear almost red as the explosions light up the twilight. The first victims of the surprise attack were the fighters of the VVS's 15th Fighter Aviation Regiment, assigned to the Baltic Special Military District's 8th Mixed Aviation Division. Like most other VVS airfields, Alytus had not been alerted when the attack arrived, and due to Stalin's concern that any preparations might provoke a German attack, lacked effective antiaircraft defenses and did not have its aircraft dispersed or camouflaged. The regiment's newly received 62 new MiG-3 fighters were parked in neat rows on the airfield along with the unit's old I-15bis and I-153 fighters. Richthofen's Bf 110s employed their forward-firing two 20mm cannon and four 7.92 machine guns and bombloads against the MiGs, setting 40 of the new fighters ablaze. Luftwaffe aircraft heavily employed SD-2 high-explosive bomblets, devastatingly effective against aircraft parked in the open, during attacks on Soviet airfields during Operation *Barbarossa*.

Keller's Luftflotte 1 had three Geschwaderen of Ju 88 As, but lacked any other strike aircraft, and had to employ them in costly low-level attacks against counterattacking Soviet mechanized forces in the first few days of the invasion. (Getty Images)

in small, squadron-sized units of 12 or fewer aircraft without fighter escort. Most squadrons tried to attack from 3,000 to 4,000m (9,842ft–13,123ft) according to their prewar training, while others approached at low 900–1,000m (2,952ft–3,280ft) altitudes, increasing their vulnerability to enemy antiaircraft fire. The VVS pilots typically held their courses, not taking evasive action when attacked by flak or enemy fighters. Luftflotte 2 commander Kesselring described the VVS attacks as "infanticide," and the Bf 109s began to report large numbers of kills. By noon, the Luftwaffe's leading ace, JG 51 commander Werner Mölders, had downed three SBs, raising his score to 72.

As the frontal bomber divisions launched their costly attacks, the Soviet long-range bomber force (DBA), based too far to the east to have been hit by the Luftwaffe's initial strikes, remained inactive. After ten hours, the DBA bombers were ordered to attack in the early afternoon, although the unit commissars insisted on a further delay to prepare the crews with political lectures before takeoff. The DBA bomber raids also lacked fighter escorts, and the DB-3s proved just as vulnerable as the SBs. Twenty-two of 70 DB-3Fs of the 96 DBAP (Long-Range Bomber Aviation Regiment) of the 3 BAK (Bomber Aviation Corps) failed to return from their first mission, with many others heavily damaged.

The Luftwaffe's surprise assault had inflicted massive losses on the VVS. Göring received reports that 1,489 Soviet aircraft had been destroyed on the ground, a figure so high he dispatched teams to verify the result. The surveys ultimately recorded a total of over 2,000 wrecks littering the VVS's airbases. The Western Special Military District suffered the heaviest losses of the day. The 9 SAD lost 347 of 409 aircraft destroyed, including most of its 57 MiG-3s along with 52 I-16s. Its commander, General Sergey Chernykh, a Hero of the Soviet Union and the first pilot to shoot down a Bf 109 while serving in Spain, was soon arrested and executed by the NKVD. The district's 10 Mixed Aviation Division lost 180 of 231 aircraft, and the 11 SAD lost 127 of 199. The larger VVS component in the Kiev Special Military District to the south fared better, with many of its airfields farther from the border and more action taken in the early morning hours to increase readiness. In total, the Kiev district lost 192 aircraft on the first day out of its initial force of 1,913. Further south, VVS Odessa Special Military District Commander General Fyodor Michugin had taken the initiative to alert his forces and disperse his aircraft, so he lost only 23 aircraft to the June 22 attacks by Fliegerkorps IV and the Romanian Air Force.

An SB crew ready for nighttime operations. The devastating losses suffered during daytime operations led Soviet long-range DBA and frontal bomber forces to operate during the hours of darkness whenever possible. The lack of Luftwaffe night fighters on the Eastern Front reduced losses, although the accuracy of Soviet bombing decreased dramatically. (From the fonds of the RGAKFD in Krasnogorsk via Stavka)

The Soviets flew as many as 6,000 sorties during the day, but while they often fought tenaciously, they lost heavily in air engagements with the veteran Bf 109 pilots. The Luftwaffe claimed a total of 322 kills in the air, and the VVS itself reported 336 losses. JG 53 claimed the highest number of kills during the day, 74, while JG 54 in East Prussia claimed 45 aerial victories along with 35 VVS aircraft destroyed on the ground. JG 51 claimed 12 Soviet fighters and 57 bombers shot down, plus 129 VVS aircraft destroyed on the ground. SKG 210 had the highest claims against ground targets, reporting 344 destroyed on the ground in attacks on 14 airfields at a cost of seven Bf 110s destroyed or damaged.

In contrast, the Luftwaffe and its Romanian allies suffered minor losses. All three of the attacking air fleets lost a total of 24 Bf 109s, 23 Ju 88s, 11 He 111s, seven Bf 110s, two Stukas, and a single Do 17, although additional aircraft received major battle damage. In its support to Luftwaffe attacks in the south against Soviet forces in Bessarabia, Romania lost four Blenheims, two PZL P.37s, two Savoia-Marchetti 79 Bs, one Potez 633, one IAR 33, and one IAR 3. With additional miscellaneous aircraft lost during the day, Axis losses approached 90 aircraft in total.

The aerial battles of the first day set the pattern for 1941 air combat in the east. Flying their speedy Bf 109s, the veteran Luftwaffe pilots used their radios to orchestrate their Rotte and Schwarm two- and four-ship formations in repeated slashing attacks against Soviet bombers or fighters flying in tight three-plane Vics. VVS bombers typically flew on doggedly despite the attacks until shot down, while the fighters often scattered to be picked off by the faster German fighters. Many Soviet airmen fought with desperate bravery, and June 22 saw the first "taran" ramming attacks against Luftwaffe aircraft. Tarans harked back to a famous action in Russian aviation history when P.N. Nesterov rammed and destroyed an Austro-Hungarian aircraft in August 1914. Lieutenant Dmitry Kokorev of the 124 IAP of the 9 SAD made the first reported taran in 1941, ramming his MiG-3's propeller into a

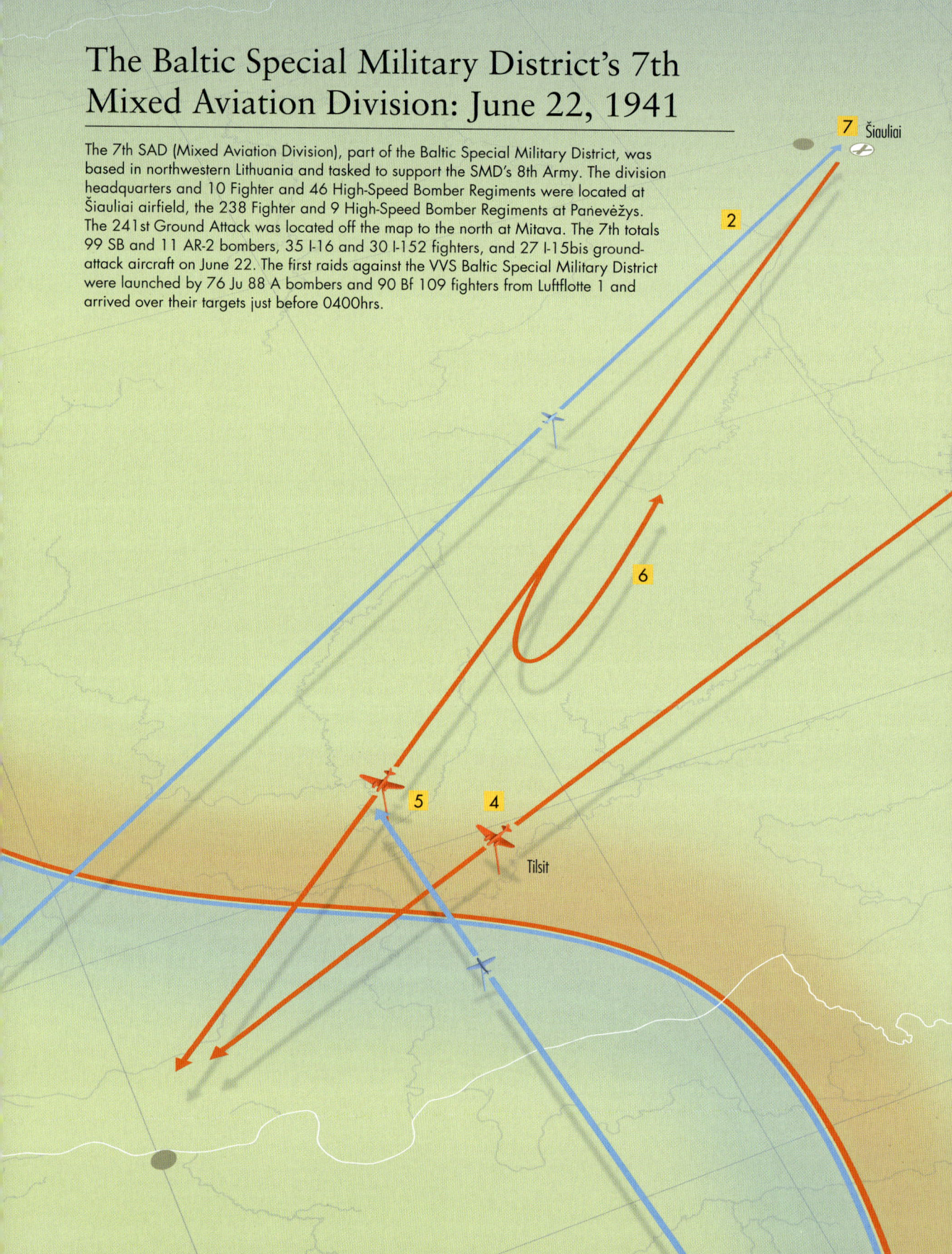

The Baltic Special Military District's 7th Mixed Aviation Division: June 22, 1941

The 7th SAD (Mixed Aviation Division), part of the Baltic Special Military District, was based in northwestern Lithuania and tasked to support the SMD's 8th Army. The division headquarters and 10 Fighter and 46 High-Speed Bomber Regiments were located at Šiauliai airfield, the 238 Fighter and 9 High-Speed Bomber Regiments at Panevėžys. The 241st Ground Attack was located off the map to the north at Mitava. The 7th totals 99 SB and 11 AR-2 bombers, 35 I-16 and 30 I-152 fighters, and 27 I-15bis ground-attack aircraft on June 22. The first raids against the VVS Baltic Special Military District were launched by 76 Ju 88 A bombers and 90 Bf 109 fighters from Luftflotte 1 and arrived over their targets just before 0400hrs.

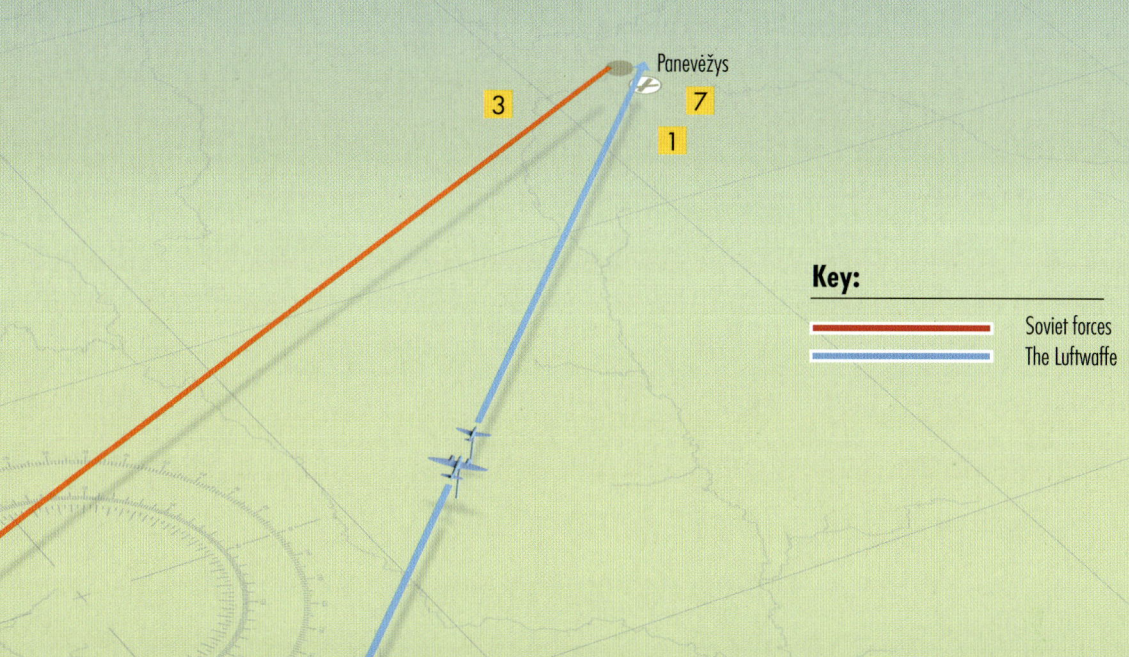

Panevėžys

Key:
— Soviet forces
— The Luftwaffe

EVENTS

1. JG 54 Bf 109s and KG 76 Ju 88 As attack Panevėžys in the first wave, catching the 9 SBAP's 52 SB bombers lined up along the runway for training, along with the I-16s and I-15bis fighters of the 238 IAP. With only a single Soviet machine gun firing to defend the airfield, the Ju 88s fly over at 30m (98ft) and devastate the parked aircraft by releasing hundreds of SD-2 fragmentation bombs, followed by strafing runs by the Bf 109s. Twenty-one of the SBs are put out of action.

2. Nine Bf 109s strafe Šiauliai airfield, damaging some of the hangars and airfield facilities.

3. Fighters take off from Soviet bases, but with orders to try and force any German aircraft encountered to land. VVS Baltic Special Military District Commander orders immediate counterattacks launched against targets in enemy territory. In response, 25 9 SBAP SBs take off from Panevėžys at 0450hrs.

4. Led by Captain Mikhail Krivtsov, the SBs drop their bombs on the railyard in Tilsit from 7,500m (24,606ft) and return to base without being intercepted.

5. At 0538hrs, a second raid of 18 SBs from 46 SBAP takes off from Šiauliai to strike German troop concentrations near Tilsit. II./JG 53 and 9./JG 54 Bf 109s intercept them, shooting down ten SBs. One Bf 109, piloted by Lieutenant Waldemar Wübke, is shot down by the SB's gunners. Wübke, one of the top aces of the Luftwaffe at the time with 37 victories, regains German lines several days later but dies of his wounds.

6. On receipt of new orders not to cross the state boundary, the 5th Squadron of the 46 SBAP returns to base without dropping its bombs.

7. SAD bases are repeatedly raided by Luftwaffe aircraft throughout the day, and the division loses a total of 90 aircraft, 20 of these shot down by German flak or Bf 109s and the rest on the ground. The VVS Baltic SMD loses a total of 479 aircraft on June 22, 379 destroyed or abandoned on the ground. The Luftwaffe loses seven aircraft destroyed and 19 damaged.

KG 2 Do 17's stabilizer when he ran out of ammunition. Kokorev downed the bomber and was able to survive by crash-landing his fighter, but many other pilots were killed during ramming attacks. A total of 19 tarans were reported for June 22, although some were probably near-misses or actual shoot-downs rather than true ramming attacks. Although most tarans were conducted during the conflict's early desperate months, Soviet pilots would continue to attempt to ram enemy aircraft throughout the war. Bombers were the usual target, and the VVS fighter would typically try to approach from behind, match the target's speed, damage the German's control surfaces with the propeller, and pull sharply away after contact to avoid a collision.

Barbarossa drives east
Luftflotte 2: to Minsk and Smolensk

While the Luftwaffe wreaked havoc on the VVS's airbases during the first hours of June 22, the Wehrmacht's four panzer groups penetrated the weak border defenses and began to drive deep behind the frontier. Soviet military districts were redesignated as wartime fronts, and began to counterattack with their reserve mechanized corps. German reconnaissance aircraft identified additional Soviet airfields over the next few days, and a total of 123 bases were struck by Luftwaffe raids. By June 25, the German airmen found few Soviet airfields in the forward area worth attacking and the Luftflotten began to focus on support to the ground advance, hitting targets ahead of the panzer spearheads, screening their flanks, and striking Soviet lines of communication to isolate the battlefield. By the end of June, the Luftwaffe claimed to have destroyed 3,100 enemy aircraft and the Soviets reported 3,922 lost. The Luftwaffe suffered 276 aircraft destroyed and 208 damaged by enemy action, with an additional 209 lost to accidents. High-tempo operations and difficulties flying supplies up to advanced bases began to impact readiness, with the Luftwaffe reduced to 458 sorties on June 28 and 260 the next day.

Soviet command structure June–July, 1941				
Special Military District	Front (June 22)	Front commander	Initial VVS commander	Subsequent VVS commander
Leningrad	Northern	M.M. Popov	A.A. Novikov	A.A. Novikov
Baltic	Northeastern	F.I. Kuznetsov	A.P. Ionov	T.T. Kutsevalov (July 1)
Western	Western	D.G. Pavlov	I.I. Kopets/A.I. Tayurskiy	N.F. Naumenko (July 2)
Kiev	Southwestern	M.P. Kirponos	Ye. S. Ptukhin	F.A. Astakov (July 1)
Odessa	Southern	Ya. T. Cherevichenko	F.G. Michugin	P.S. Sheukhin (June 27)

In the center, Kesselring's Luftflotte 2 dominated the air as Guderian's 2 and Hoth's 3 Panzer Groups drove deep behind the shattered Soviet frontlines. With landlines severed, command posts bombed, and radios jammed, Soviet Western Front Commander General D.G. Pavlov ordered his deputy, General I.V. Boldin, to fly to Białystok on June 22 to organize a counterstroke. Boldin's aircraft had to dodge several formations of Luftwaffe aircraft and found chaos and confusion on landing. By June 24, he was able to launch an attack with the 6 Cavalry, and 6 and 11 Mechanized Corps in the Grodno area, which was aimed at cutting off the advance of Generaloberst Hermann Hoth's Panzer Group 3. Richthofen's Fliegerkorps VIII threw Stukas, Hs 123s, bombers, Zerstörers, and fighter aircraft into repeated strikes on the massing cavalry and tanks, flying 500 sorties on June 25.

Wrecked Soviet aircraft at one of the bases struck on June 22, a sight familiar to German forces as they drove east into the USSR. A Ju 52 transport is in the background, likely helping to prepare the airfield to support Luftwaffe operations. (Getty Images)

The Germans claimed to have disabled 105 tanks and the 6 Cavalry Corps reported losses of 50 percent after being caught in the open by the Do 17s of KG 2.

VVS Western Front ordered its surviving SBs, reinforced with DBA bombers, to strike the panzer group spearheads, but again was unable to attach escort fighters. The Front's 9, 10, and 11 Mixed Aviation Divisions and their fighter regiments were largely destroyed on June 22, and General Georgy Zakharov's 43 IAD (Fighter Aviation Division) was held back to protect the Front headquarters in Minsk. Zakharov's fighters downed seven StG 1 and 2 Stukas over the city, but without fighter cover, the waves of bombers from the Front's 12 and 18 Bomber Aviation Divisions and DBA were unprotected. On June 24, nine of 27 DB-3s and DB-3Fs of the 53 BAP (Bomber Aviation Regiment) were lost, eight to the Bf 109s of JG 27. Fifty-eight bombers were lost the next day attempting to bomb Luftwaffe elements that had displaced forward to operate from the captured airfield at Vilnius. General Ivan Kopets, the VVS Western Front commander, killed himself on June 23 after surveying the wreckage on his airfields from the air. Kopets' deputy, General Andrei Taiurskii, assumed command, but he was arrested on July 2 and General Nikolai Naumenko was brought forward from the Leningrad Military District to take command. VVS Western Front strength plunged to 369 available aircraft on July 10.

Mölders on the Eastern Front (overleaf)

The veteran Fliegerjaeger of the Luftwaffe in their Bf 109 fighters inflicted huge losses on the VVS in the early months of the war. With the onset of the German invasion, the Soviets ordered immediate bomber strikes on the advancing panzers. Many Soviet fighters had been destroyed on their runways in the first hours of the attack, and their loss, along with command and control confusion, left most Soviet bombers unescorted when sent into the attack. Most of the raids were by squadrons of 12 or fewer bombers, which proved disastrously vulnerable to German flak and the defending Bf 109s.

On June 25, Oberst Werner Mölders, the Luftwaffe's leading ace, engaged a formation of SB-2 bombers and shot down two in short order. Within days, Mölders exceeded Manfred von Richthofen's World War I score of 80 victories, and in early July became the first fighter pilot in history to shoot down over 100 enemy aircraft.

On August 7, Mölders was appointed Inspector of Fighters, responsible for the operations and tactics of the entire Luftwaffe fighter force, but he retained command of JG 51 for several months. In November, he was killed on the flight home when recalled to Germany for the funeral of Ernst Udet.

To the south, Guderian's Panzer Group 2 advanced rapidly towards Minsk. On June 24, JG 51 pilots reported downing 64 SBs and 18 DB-3s at a cost of 11 fighters in engagements covering Guderian's panzer columns. Staffel commander Karl-Heinz Schnell reported seven victories during the day, including four SBs shot down in just two minutes. JG 51 Bf 109s flying free-hunt patrols intercepted more Soviet bombers on June 25, reporting 70 SBs destroyed at a cost of four Bf 109s. Guderian's columns had bypassed the fortress at Brest on June 22, leaving the 45 Infantry Division to capture the fortress. After several assaults were repulsed, the Luftwaffe dropped SD-500 bombs on June 28, but to little effect. Later in the day, special SD-1800 1.8-ton bombs were able to penetrate the fortress's thick brick walls, and it fell after an epic defense two days later.

On June 27, the advance guards of Army Group Center's Panzer Groups 2 and 3 met in the Minsk area encircling over 400,000 Soviet troops. Marshal S.K. Timoshenko assumed command of the Western Front after Pavlov's arrest and ordered an all-out VVS effort to destroy Guderian's crossing sites over the Berezina at Bobruysk in early July. The remains of the VVS Western Front SB force, along with the DB-3s and obsolete TB-3s of the DBA's 3 BAK, flew repeated daylight raids against the bridgehead. The bombers flew at low altitudes against the bridges, and over 100 Soviet aircraft were lost to the intense antiaircraft fire from the Luftwaffe's 10 Flak Regiment and patrolling JG 51 Bf 109s. Oberst Werner Mölders claimed five bombers during the day, surpassing Manfred von Richthofen's World War I score of 80 by bringing his victory total to 82.

Chief of OKH Halder noted in his diary on July 3 that it was "probably no overstatement to say that the Russian Campaign has been won in the space of two weeks." The Białystok and Minsk pockets collapsed on July 9, leaving the Western Front with less than 200 tanks to oppose Army Group Center. The Germans, however, had not considered the Soviet ability to bring new forces to the front, and as Army Group Center advanced on Smolensk, it encountered a line of new reserve armies while VVS Western Front was reinforced with 900 additional aircraft during July. Kesselring planned to mass both Fliegerkorps VIII and II to support a planned assault across the Dnieper on July 12, but Panzer Group 2 had made a surprise crossing the day before and was thrusting towards Smolensk to meet Hoth and create a new pocket. The VVS flew in support of Timoshenko's July 23–24 counterattack to relieve the encircled forces. Although now careful to ensure bomber sorties had fighter cover,

A three-plane "kette" of Ju 87 Stukas in flight. Richthofen's Fliegerkorps VIII used its Stukas and ground-attack aircraft effectively to thwart the Western Front's Grodno counterattack. With limited numbers of Stukas, however, Luftwaffe medium bombers were often used for low-level close support attacks. (Nik Cornish at www.stavka.photos/)

An SB fast bomber being readied for operations. The VVS attempted to support the counteroffensives by Eastern Front mechanized corps with SB and DBA DB-3 bombers, but it lost heavily to Bf 109s and the antiaircraft elements attached to the lead panzer units. (Courtesy of the Central Museum of the Armed Forces, Moscow via Stavka)

the Soviet airmen still suffered heavy losses to the Bf 109s, and 83 aircraft were lost during July 26–27 alone. By the end of the month, only 188 Soviet aircraft were left in the center to support the struggle for Smolensk: 70 with VVS West Front, 44 with the newly formed VVS Reserve Front, 12 DB-3s and 12 TB-3s with the 1 BAK, and 50 DB-3s with the 3 BAK. Luftflotte 2 flew 696 sorties on July 28, while the VVS Western Front and supporting DBA bombers could only manage 327. The bombers of Kesselring's Fliegerkorps II launched sustained strikes against Soviet lines of communications throughout the period and reported the destruction of 126 trains and 15 bridges in the final days of July.

The Luftwaffe continued to dominate in air-to-air combat as inadequately trained VVS pilots were repeatedly bounced and shot down by the veteran German airmen in their Bf 109s. Most Soviet pilots had a life expectancy of only a few weeks, even if flying new model fighters, and regiments took such heavy losses they were often pulled out for rebuilding after brief periods of operations due to losses. On July 29, JG 53 claimed its 1,000th victory of the war. The 410 OSNAZ (Special Purpose) Bomber Aviation Regiment was formed with 38 Pe-2s crewed by experienced test pilots, but it lost 33 during three weeks of operations in July. The DBA element supporting operations against Luftflotte 2, the 3 BAK, lost a total of 270 bombers between *Barbarossatag* and August 4.

Ultimately, Timoshenko was unable to relieve the armies encircled around Smolensk, although some 100,000 Soviet troops were able to escape the pocket through areas screened only by Luftflotte 2 air patrols. Army Group Center captured another 310,000 Soviet troops with the collapse of the pocket on August 5. Two days before, Hitler ordered Richthofen's Fliegerkorps VIII north to strengthen Army Group North's assault on Leningrad. Kesselring was left with only Loerzer's Fliegerkorps II to support von Bock, who was soon forced onto the defensive as his panzer groups were transferred to the north and south. Loerzer's bombers were employed extensively in strikes on the rail network as far deep as Bryansk to hinder the arrival of Soviet reinforcements, while others were diverted to strike enemy river monitors that had been interfering with Army Group Center operations along the northern portion of the Pripyat Marshes.

Luftflotte 1: the drive through the Baltics

Like von Bock's troops, von Leeb's Army Group North rapidly penetrated Soviet border defenses on June 22. General Erich von Manstein's 56 Panzer Korps crossed the Dvina River at Daugavpils on June 26, and VVS Northwestern Front commander General Aleksey Ionov threw his bombers against the bridgehead. As in the Army Group Center sector, the attacks by squadron-sized units without fighter escort provided easy targets for the veteran Bf 109 pilots, and on June 23, JG 54 filed claims for 39 victories and reported only three losses. The VVS fought intensely, and three Ju 88s were lost to ramming attacks while five aircraft from the navy's VVS Baltic Fleet crashed their damaged aircraft into enemy ground columns

OPPOSITE THE COURSE OF AIR OPERATIONS, JUNE 22 TO AUGUST, 1941

in what became known as "fire tarans." While the battles near the frontier raged, DBA and frontal aviation bombers were dispatched in small-scale and costly raids against targets in German territory. The DBA's 7 DBAP lost three DB-3s in a raid on Königsberg and the 46 SBAP lost 13 SBs and Ar-2s attacking Gumbinnen, although the victorious 54 JG Bf 109s also downed three Ju 88s mistaken for SBs during the confused fighting.

The Northwestern Front's commander, General Fyodor Kuznetsov, launched his 3 and 12 Mechanized Corps in a counterattack against the 41 Panzer Korps as it drove inland from the border. Keller's Luftflotte 1 again employed their Ju 88s in low-level runs against the counterattacking Soviet forces. The Red Army's light T-26 tanks proved vulnerable to air attack, and strikes on supply convoys left hundreds of Soviet tanks and vehicles stranded without fuel. In the 28 Tank Division alone, 198 tanks were left abandoned. On July 1, Keller was reinforced by 40 ZG 26 Bf 110s transferred from Army Group Center to assist with close-support missions.

By the end of June, Kuznetsov's counterattacks had been shattered and Army Group North's divisions advanced rapidly through Latvia. Desperately short of reconnaissance aircraft, the Soviets were surprised to discover that a panzer division had captured a bridgehead at Ostrov. As Keller's units began to displace forward, they found the captured airfields crowded with destroyed or abandoned VVS aircraft, including 86 wrecks at Kaunas airfield and 57 at Vilnius. Ivanov's VVS Northwestern Front had lost 425 aircraft on the ground and 465 in the air by the end of June. The vulnerable SBs suffered especially heavily, and of 403 in the VVS Baltic Military District at the start of the war, 205 were shot down and 148 were destroyed on the ground. The Soviets were forced to draw regiments from General Mikhail Samokhin's VVS Baltic Fleet and General Alexander Novikov's VVS Northern Front to contest the air over the Baltic States.

Novikov's forces were thinly stretched as his VVS Northern Front was responsible not only for defending the southern approaches to Leningrad, but also covering the Finnish border all the way to the Barents Sea. Novikov was one of the few senior VVS leaders to survive the first period of the war and would lead the VVS to victory from 1942 to 1945, but he suffered the same heavy losses as his compatriots when throwing unsupported bombers against the Luftwaffe. On July 6, Novikov's bomber regiments attacked the Ostrov bridgehead and lost 62 aircraft to JG 54's Bf 109 patrols. The next day, JG 54 claimed another 42 victories at the cost of ten Bf 109s destroyed or damaged, pushing the Geschwader to over 750 victory claims. During the first ten days of July, Novikov's airmen had flown 1,200 sorties and dropped 226kg (500lb) of bombs on Panzer Group 4's columns on the roads leading to Ostrov, but at the cost of most of his bomber force. Novikov learned quickly and ordered his fighters to avoid engaging the Bf 109s and concentrate on attacks against Luftwaffe bombers and reconnaissance aircraft. On July 3, his fighters shot down five Ju 88s followed by three more on each of the next two days. To limit bomber losses, Novikov directed more operations at night to exploit the Luftwaffe's lack of night fighters on the Eastern Front.

Panzer Group 4 reached Luga in mid-July, only 96km (60 miles) from Leningrad. On July 14, Novikov was able to concentrate 235 aircraft, including units from the 2 SAD and bombers from the 1 BAK to support a counterattack by the Soviet 11 Army against von Manstein's 56 Panzer Korps near Soltsy. Luftflotte 1's fighters had yet to displace to forward airfields, limiting the time Bf 109s could operate over the front, and Novikov managed 1,500 close-support sorties during the four-day battle. The 8 Panzer Division suffered heavy losses and was driven from its forward positions. By mid-July, Panzer Group 4 regrouped to consolidate its hold on the Luga River while Leeb's 18 Army cleared Estonia on the left

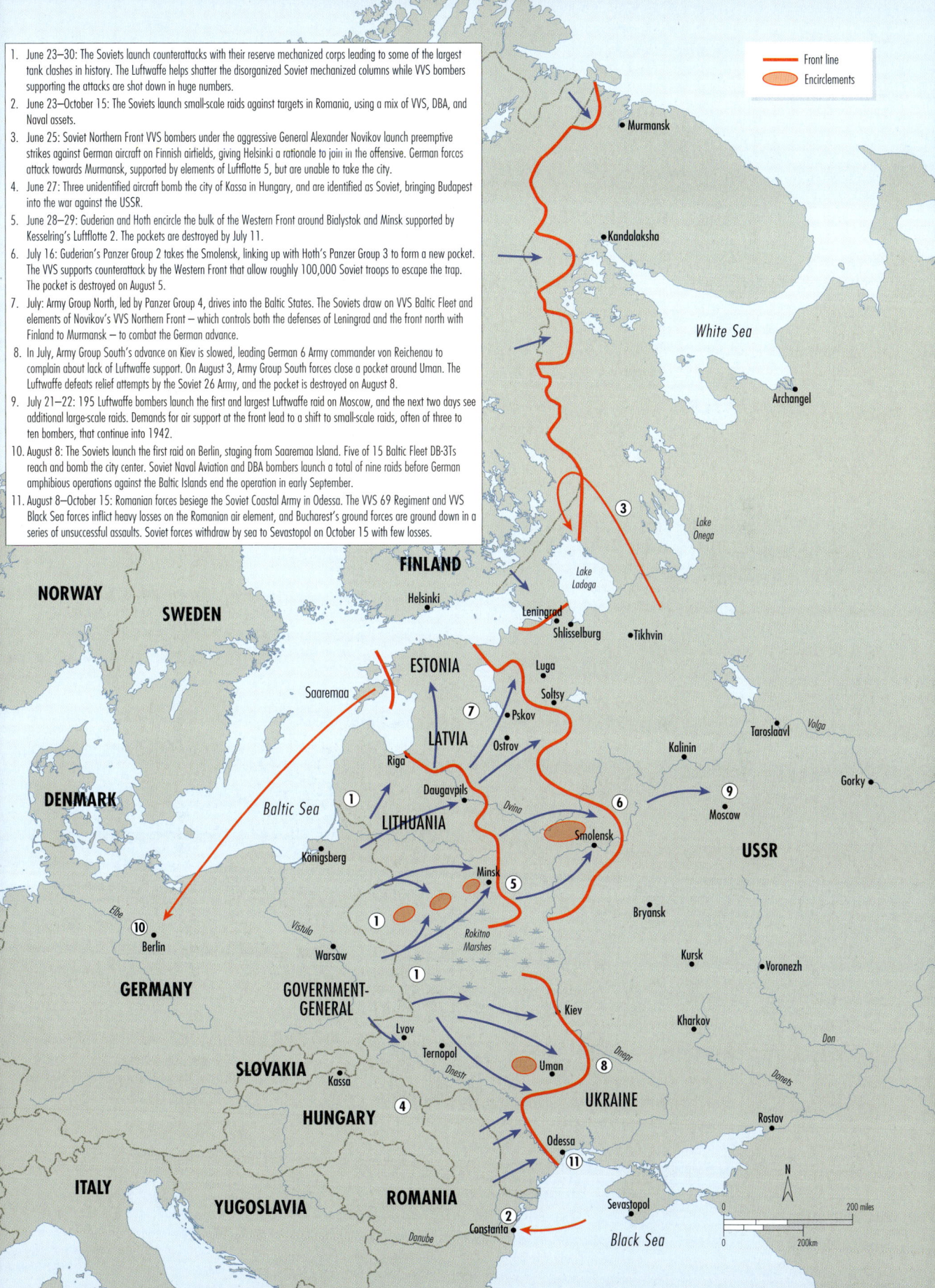

1. June 23–30: The Soviets launch counterattacks with their reserve mechanized corps leading to some of the largest tank clashes in history. The Luftwaffe helps shatter the disorganized Soviet mechanized columns while VVS bombers supporting the attacks are shot down in huge numbers.
2. June 23–October 15: The Soviets launch small-scale raids against targets in Romania, using a mix of VVS, DBA, and Naval assets.
3. June 25: Soviet Northern Front VVS bombers under the aggressive General Alexander Novikov launch preemptive strikes against German aircraft on Finnish airfields, giving Helsinki a rationale to join in the offensive. German forces attack towards Murmansk, supported by elements of Luftflotte 5, but are unable to take the city.
4. June 27: Three unidentified aircraft bomb the city of Kassa in Hungary, and are identified as Soviet, bringing Budapest into the war against the USSR.
5. June 28–29: Guderian and Hoth encircle the bulk of the Western Front around Bialystok and Minsk supported by Kesselring's Luftflotte 2. The pockets are destroyed by July 11.
6. July 16: Guderian's Panzer Group 2 takes the Smolensk, linking up with Hoth's Panzer Group 3 to form a new pocket. The VVS supports counterattack by the Western Front that allow roughly 100,000 Soviet troops to escape the trap. The pocket is destroyed on August 5.
7. July: Army Group North, led by Panzer Group 4, drives into the Baltic States. The Soviets draw on VVS Baltic Fleet and elements of Novikov's VVS Northern Front — which controls both the defenses of Leningrad and the front north with Finland to Murmansk — to combat the German advance.
8. In July, Army Group South's advance on Kiev is slowed, leading German 6 Army commander von Reichenau to complain about lack of Luftwaffe support. On August 3, Army Group South forces close a pocket around Uman. The Luftwaffe defeats relief attempts by the Soviet 26 Army, and the pocket is destroyed on August 8.
9. July 21–22: 195 Luftwaffe bombers launch the first and largest Luftwaffe raid on Moscow, and the next two days see additional large-scale raids. Demands for air support at the front lead to a shift to small-scale raids, often of three to ten bombers, that continue into 1942.
10. August 8: The Soviets launch the first raid on Berlin, staging from Saaremaa Island. Five of 15 Baltic Fleet DB-3Ts reach and bomb the city center. Soviet Naval Aviation and DBA bombers launch a total of nine raids before German amphibious operations against the Baltic Islands end the operation in early September.
11. August 8–October 15: Romanian forces besiege the Soviet Coastal Army in Odessa. The VVS 69 Regiment and VVS Black Sea forces inflict heavy losses on the Romanian air element, and Bucharest's ground forces are ground down in a series of unsuccessful assaults. Soviet forces withdraw by sea to Sevastopol on October 15 with few losses.

A downed Soviet MiG-3 fighter. Although it had a powerful engine and performed well at high altitudes, the MiG-3 was sluggish at the medium and lower altitudes where most Eastern Front air combat took place. VVS MiG-3 units lost heavily, and production was curtailed in early 1942. (Wiki Commons)

and the 16 Army advanced to maintain communications with Army Group Center on the right. By the end of the month, Keller's Luftflotte 1 was reduced to 350 operational aircraft.

Luftflotte 4: into the Ukraine

While German forces advanced rapidly north of the Pripyat Marshes, Rundstedt's Army Group South made slower progress towards Kiev, its initial objective. Due to Stalin's belief that the primary German axis of advance would be into Ukraine, the commander of the Southwestern Front, General Mikhail Kirponos, had the strongest of the four border military districts and commanded eight mechanized corps. Kirponos's airmen were led by General Yevgeniy Ptukin, a Hero of the Soviet Union and veteran of the Spanish Civil War and the 1939–40 war with Finland. His VVS Southwestern Front had lost fewer aircraft on June 22 than the other military districts, but as Kirponos began to launch counterattacks, Ptukin decided to shift his headquarters to join the Front HQ at Tarnopol, disrupting command and control during the move. With landline communications severed and radios jammed, Ptukin was reduced to dispatching U-2 biplanes to deliver written orders. Ptukin was arrested on charges of sabotage on June 24 and replaced by General Fyodor Astakhov.

Like Kesselring's and Keller's air fleets, Loehr kept up the pressure on Soviet airfields for several days after *Barbarossatag*. From June 22–25, Luftflotte 4 hit 77 enemy airfields with roughly 1,600 sorties, reporting 774 aircraft destroyed on the ground, while JG 3 claimed 89 enemy aircraft destroyed in the air. The 14 and 15 Mixed Aviation Divisions reported losses of 129 and 166 aircraft, respectively. VVS and DBA bombers attempted to strike the German columns, and MiG-3s were sent on strafing runs. On June 23, after 27 bombers from BAK 4 were lost on a single mission, the survivors encountered weeping family members when they returned to base, a situation seen at other DBA airfields before civilians were evacuated to rear areas.

The advance to contact of Kirponos's mechanized corps was closely tracked by German reconnaissance aircraft, and Loehr sent in the bombers of Fliegerkorps V's KGs 51, 54, and 55 in low-level attacks against the attacking mechanized corps. The strikes were effective but costly, with 22 aircraft lost on June 26 including eight He 111s and Ju 88s shot down and nine damaged. KG 51 was reduced from 92 to 37 Ju 88s by the end of the month. The reconnaissance aircraft gave German commanders a critical advantage, but at a cost. From June 22 to July 25, 92 Army Group South reconnaissance aircraft assigned at the army level or to Fliegerkorps V had been destroyed or damaged, 55 of these total losses.

20mm quad antiaircraft gun. The German ground forces advancing into the USSR were provided with capable light and medium antiaircraft artillery, and VVS aircraft attempting to attack at low levels often took heavy losses. VVS attacks on German bridgeheads, which were well protected by flak, were particularly costly. (Nik Cornish at www.stavka.photos/)

A small-scale airstrike with major implications for *Barbarossa* took place on June 26 when three bombers attacked the Hungarian city of Kassa. Hungary had signed the Tripartite Pact in 1940, but although it had mobilized its air and air defense assets, it was reluctant to join the attack on the USSR. An unexploded Soviet-manufactured FAB-100 bomb was identified at the scene, leading Budapest to declare war on the Soviet Union on the 27th. Although it retained significant troops to watch Romania, some of its best units were formed into the Hungarian Carpathian Corps and sent to join the offensive in July. Disoriented Soviet bomber crews were likely responsible and the raid on Kassa a tragic mistake, although the USSR asserted it was a deliberate provocation operation conducted by three Romanian P.37 bombers. If it was indeed a clandestine operation designed to push Hungary into joining the invasion, it would rank as one of the most successful in history, with the result that Kirponos had to defend a wider front.

By the end of June, the Southwestern Front's mechanized counterattacks had been repulsed with the loss of 200,000 troops, and Kirponos ordered the evacuation of Lvov. Soviet forces began to retreat towards Kiev and the Dnieper River. The VVS Southwestern Front had also taken devastating losses attempting to support the counteroffensive, losing 1,500 of its initial force of 1,900 aircraft, including 58 of the new MiG-3 fighters. By the evening of June 26, the VVS Southwestern Front only had 284 operational aircraft including 26 SBs, 18 Pe-2s, 117 I-153s, 68 I-16s, 20 MiG-3s, and 35 Yak-1s.

Loehr now concentrated on attacking the rail network west of the Dnieper River to disrupt Kirponos's retreat. On July 6, Luftflotte 4 flew 260 sorties and claimed 250 trucks, 11 tanks, and six trains destroyed, while JG 3 fighters shot down 41 aircraft from the 46 Mixed Aviation Division and 4 BAK while only losing one Bf 109. The Soviets even sent obsolete TB-3s into the attempt to defend Kiev, and on July 10 a Rotte of Bf 109s on a free-hunt patrol came upon 12 of the four-engine bombers and downed five. By early July, the Luftwaffe had effectively shut down Soviet rail movement west of the Dnieper, and numerous trains were cut off and abandoned along the lines. Despite the successful interdiction operations, the Luftwaffe found itself under intense pressure from Heer commanders, in particular Field Marshal Walther von Reichenau, the commander of 6 Army, for more close-air support. Greim was heavily committed to supporting the attack of Panzer Group 1 and the 17 Army

Il-2 Shturmoviks on an operation. The superb Il-2 ground-attack aircraft had a limited impact on operations in 1941, as it only reached the force in small numbers and the ground-attack regiments were still in the process of developing effective tactics. In 1942, the availability of larger numbers of Shturmoviks and the production of the Il-2M with a rear gunner would allow the aircraft to make a critical contribution to Soviet success on the battlefield. (Getty Images)

towards Uman, and with only a single fighter Geschwader, JG 3, to cover the huge area of operations, he had few resources available for Reichenau. On July 6, Loehr organized a close-support task force, *Nahkampfluherer Nord*, to improve close-support operations. JG 3's commander, Major Günther Lützow, was appointed to lead the organization, and was given 77 Ju 87s and 40 Bf 109s drawn from StG 77, JG 3, and JG 53. Additional JG 52 Bf 109s were detached from General Hans Speidel's force guarding Romanian oil facilities to reinforce Lutzow on July 31.

In Bessarabia, air operations began on June 22, although the German 11 Army stationed in Romania did not begin its ground offensive until July 2. The air struggle pitted Loehr's Fliegerkorps IV, led by General Kurt Pflugbeil, and the Romanian air force against the VVS Southern Front. Despite the vague and contradictory orders from Moscow, General F.G. Michugin had alerted his forces before the first raids struck. Only 23 of his aircraft were destroyed on the ground on June 22, leaving the Axis airmen to face 827 Southern Front aircraft, 706 of them operational, along with 626 VVS Black Sea Fleet aircraft stationed along the Black Sea Coast. Air combat over Bessarabia was as intense as to the north, and through to the end of July, the Romanian Air force flew 5,100 sorties, 2,162 by fighters, and claimed 88 kills at a cost of 58 aircraft. During the fighting, a MiG-3 flown by Lieutenant Aleksandr Pokryshkin shot down a PZL P.24, the first victory scored by the pilot who would end the war as the second-highest scoring Allied ace with 59 victories.

With Kirponos's forces digging in to defend Kiev and the line of the Dnieper River, von Rundstedt directed Kleist's Panzer Group 1 to angle its advance to the southeast, leaving Reichenau's 6 Army to advance alone against Kiev. The German 11 Army and Romanian forces, supported by Fliegerkorps IV, had driven the Soviet Southern Front from Bessarabia in July, and although the VVS Southern Front claimed 154 victories, it had been ground down to 190 fighter, 55 bomber, and 12 ground-attack aircraft when it withdrew across the Dnieper. Soviet fighters nevertheless scored a notable victory in the air on July 22 when I-16s escorting a flight of Su-2s shot down a Bf 109 flown by the notorious Nazi SS leader Reinhard Heydrich, flying with II./JG 77 as a volunteer pilot. Heydrich successfully regained German lines but was forbidden from any future combat flight operations.

On August 3, German forces linked up to seal off the Soviet 6 and 12 Armies at Uman. Stung by ground commanders' complaints about lack of support, Greim sent his Fliegerkorps V aircraft into intense attacks against Soviet forces attempting to relieve the pocket despite clouds, high winds, and rain. At the same time, Fliegerkorps IV concentrated on hitting the trapped units. The Uman pocket yielded 103,054 prisoners and 317 tanks, 818 artillery pieces, and 5,286 other motor vehicles either destroyed or captured. VVS Southern Front aviation's attempts to intervene failed, and by August 10, the Front reported total losses of 1,620 aircraft to enemy action and 242 to accidents since the beginning of the war.

A Focke-Wulf Fw 189 reconnaissance aircraft. In addition to strategic reconnaissance aircraft controlled by the Luftwaffe, a large number of tactical recon aircraft were directly controlled by ground force armies as well as some panzer divisions, giving German maneuver commanders a much greater ability to track battlefield developments than their Soviet counterparts. (Nik Cornish at www.stavka.photos/)

Soviet Raids against Romania

While Army Group South battled the Red Army's Southern and Southwestern Fronts for the Ukraine, the USSR launched a series of small-scale attacks against Romanian targets. On June 23, 49 DB-3Ts from the VVS Black Sea Fleet's 2 MTAP (Mine and Torpedo Aviation Regiment) and 24 SBs from the fleet's 40 High-Speed Bomber Regiment dropped 53.3 tons of bombs on the port of Constanța at a cost of 16 bombers lost. Lieutenant Agerici of the Romanian Air Force became an early hero, shooting down three DB-3s in his Hurricane. The next day, 18 DB-3s and 18 SBs returned to bomb the port, with another ten bombers shot down. Two days later, the Soviets used a raid by Black Sea Fleet SBs as a diversion to allow a Black Sea Fleet cruiser and two destroyers to shell Constanța. JG 52 fighters intercepted the raid and shot down seven of the 17 SBs while the destroyer *Moskva* was sunk by a mine and the destroyer *Kharkov* was damaged by coastal artillery fire.

The Soviets continued operations against Romania over the next several months, and as losses were heavy due to the effective Axis fighter and antiaircraft defenses, the Black Sea Fleet began to employ their small force of unique Zveno bombers to launch harassment raids. The Zveno TB-3 bombers carried one I-16SPB fighter bomber under each wing and released them near the target. On July 26, two of the bombers released four of the fighters for a raid on Constanța that hit docks and oil tanks at the cost of one I-16SPB lost. The Soviets sustained Zveno and small-scale raids with other aircraft against Romanian targets through August, with the last launched on October 15 to cover the evacuation of Odessa. In total, Axis sources recorded 95 Soviet raids conducted by 336 aircraft. Most were flown in daylight hours due to the lack of training for night operations, and Axis forces claimed to have destroyed 81 Soviet aircraft. Damage to Romanian facilities was minimal, in part due to the use of staged fires and dummy facilities to divert Soviet attacks.

The Siege of Odessa

While Army Group South advanced to the north, Hitler's Romanian allies focused their operations against Odessa to advance Bucharest's territorial ambitions in the east and limit the ability of the Soviet Black Sea Fleet to attack Romanian coastal targets. The Romanian 4th Army's operations against the city began on August 8, supported by the Gruparea Aeriană de Luptă (GAL). The defending Soviet Coastal Army had only weak air support, consisting of a few VVS Black Sea Fleet MBR-2 flying boat and SB bomber squadrons, and the 20 VVS I-16s of Mayor Lev Shestakov's 69 Fighter Regiment. The GAL's Bf 109 Es, Heinkel He 112s, Hurricanes, and Romanian-designed IAR 80s and 81s were all superior to the

OPPOSITE SOVIET ZVENO OPERATIONS

A German flak position in Romania. A combined force of antiaircraft troops and Bf 109 defensive fighters under General Speidel was stationed in Romania to defend the oilfields and related infrastructure from Soviet attack. (Nik Cornish at www.stavka.photos/)

In July, the Soviets turned to the unique TB-3 Zveno bomber weapon system for strikes against Romania. Originally designed to serve as an airborne aircraft carrier able to carry as many as five biplane defensive fighters, by 1941 the Zveno consisted of the obsolete TB-3 launching two I-16SPB dive bombers each carrying 250kg (551lb) FAB bombs. Three bombers and six of the fighters were formed into the 2nd Squadron of the 32 IAP/VVS/ChF. (Wiki Commons)

Soviet I-16s. By late August, however, Romanian land forces had suffered 27,000 casualties after several unsuccessful attacks on the port's defenses. The outnumbered I-16s scored a number of victories, with Shestakov personally claiming six kills. By late August, the GAL had lost a third of its aircraft, and Shestakov's I-16s were able to begin strafing enemy supply lines. The GAL was reduced to 176 aircraft by September 2, 91 of them serviceable. By late September, the besiegers had suffered 60,000 casualties and the GAL was reduced to night operations. Shestakov intercepted and shot down six Ju 52s and three gliders flying supplies to the besiegers on September 28.

By October, the collapse of Kirponos's defenses around Kiev forced the Stavka to concentrate forces for the defense of Sevastopol, and the Odessa garrison was ordered to evacuate. The Axis had been unable to control the Black Sea, with only small Romanian and Bulgarian and no German naval assets available in 1941, while maritime missions were a secondary task for Plugiel's heavily committed Fliegerkorps IV. Only one ship was lost during the October 14 evacuation and 350,000 soldiers and 200,000 tons of material were successfully transported to Sevastopol. The 64-day siege of Odessa was a rare Soviet 1941 defensive success. At a cost of 16,578 killed and 24,650 wounded, the Soviets had ultimately inflicted over 100,000 Romanian casualties and the GAL was so depleted it was withdrawn from active operations for almost a year. The highly successful 69 Fighter Regiment claimed 94 kills during the siege and later in the war, redesignated the 9 Guards Fighter Regiment, was manned with experienced pilots and in 1942 operated on the Stalingrad front as an elite "regiment of aces."

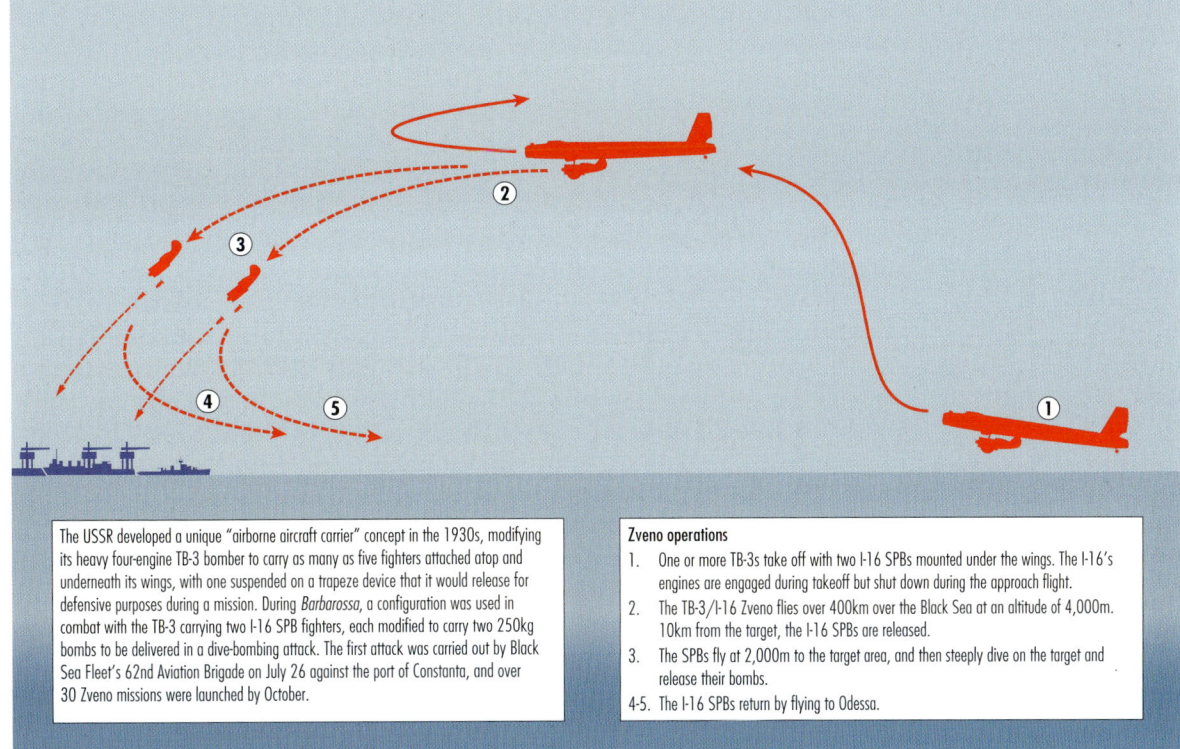

The USSR developed a unique "airborne aircraft carrier" concept in the 1930s, modifying its heavy four-engine TB-3 bomber to carry as many as five fighters attached atop and underneath its wings, with one suspended on a trapeze device that it would release for defensive purposes during a mission. During *Barbarossa*, a configuration was used in combat with the TB-3 carrying two I-16 SPB fighters, each modified to carry two 250kg bombs to be delivered in a dive-bombing attack. The first attack was carried out by Black Sea Fleet's 62nd Aviation Brigade on July 26 against the port of Constanta, and over 30 Zveno missions were launched by October.

Zveno operations
1. One or more TB-3s take off with two I-16 SPBs mounted under the wings. The I-16's engines are engaged during takeoff but shut down during the approach flight.
2. The TB-3/I-16 Zveno flies over 400km over the Black Sea at an altitude of 4,000m. 10km from the target, the I-16 SPBs are released.
3. The SPBs fly at 2,000m to the target area, and then steeply dive on the target and release their bombs.
4–5. The I-16 SPBs return by flying to Odessa.

Operations in the far north

To the north of Leningrad, *Fliegerführer* Kirkenes, under Oberst Andreas Nielsen, supported the offensive by German mountain troops to seize Murmansk and cut rail communications with the Arctic. Nielsen commanded a mixed force of 65 Ju 88s, Ju 87s, Bf 109s, and Bf 110s drawn from Luftflotte 5 in Norway along with some support aircraft. Soviet defenses were initially controlled by the VVS Northern Fleet and VVS Northern Front. Poor flying weather kept Nielsen's aircraft grounded for the first days of the campaign, and on June 25, the aggressive VVS Northern Front commander, General A.A. Novikov, began several days of air strikes intended to destroy German aircraft based in Finland. Little damage was inflicted on the Luftwaffe, and 23 Soviet aircraft were lost on the first day alone. Helsinki used the airstrikes as a rationale to openly join the campaign against the USSR. Over the next few weeks, Nielsen's bombers raided Murmansk, but the Soviet antiaircraft batteries were so effective that the attacking pilots considered the city one of the four most difficult targets they faced: the "two Ls," London and Leningrad, and the "two Ms," Malta and Murmansk.

General Eduard Dietl's XIX Mountain Corps began to attack over the barren Arctic terrain towards Murmansk on June 29, and Stuka strikes on Soviet bunkers were critical to helping maintain the pace of the advance. The Soviets retaliated by attacking Dietl's vulnerable supply lines, with MBR-2 flying boats raiding the harbors and SBs of the 137 Bomber Aviation Regiment, sinking some of the coastal freighters bringing in supplies for the mountain troops. When German and Finnish troops initiated an additional attack to the south against Kandalaksha, Nielsen lacked enough aircraft to adequately support both offensives. With the decline in Luftwaffe air opposition, the Northern Fleet was able to conduct a series of diversionary landings against Dietl's northern flank and destroyers shelled German supply lines. Eventually, the attacking Axis forces were halted and dug in short of both Murmansk and Kandalaksha, and there would be little movement from these positions for the next three years. IV.(St)/LG 1 lost 25 of its original force of 36 Stukas, but the Bf 109s attained their normal high kill ratio, shooting down 77 Soviet aircraft for the loss of eight German fighters by the end of July.

To support its new ally, Britain mounted a strike operation from the carriers *Furious* and *Victorious* on July 30. The raiders found the harbor at Petsamo empty, but lost an Albacore and two Fulmars to flak. At Kirkenes, Bf 109s and Bf 110s intercepted the attack by 20 Albacores and nine Fulmars, shooting down 11 and two, respectively. Additional help from the Allies arrived as the front stabilized in August. Forty-eight P-40 Tomahawks arrived with the first Allied supply convoy to Murmansk and were sent south to strengthen the Moscow defenses. Thirty-nine Hawker Hurricane IIBs came in the same convoy along with pilots from the RAF's 81 and 134 Squadrons to help familiarize their allies with the aircraft. On October 12, convoy PQ-1 arrived with additional P-40s. By the end of the year, a total of eight convoys with 55 ships had docked at Murmansk. With the stalemate at Murmansk and Kandalaksha, the Luftwaffe tried to cut the Kirov railway running south from Murmansk to the south with airstrikes, but Soviet rail maintenance units rapidly repaired any damage.

The war in the north had been waged with limited forces and ended in stalemate. The cost had been high, with 221 Soviet aircraft lost between June and November, 107 in air combat. Luftflotte 5 reported 89 aircraft lost or severely damaged, 44 to Soviet fighters, 21 to antiaircraft fire, and 23 to unknown causes. By December, Soviet air units in polar regions were stronger than in June 1941, with new MiG-3s, and Hurricane and P-40 fighters from the Allies. German certainty that the campaign would be over in a matter of weeks, along with Luftflotte 5 Commander Stumpf's view that Norway was his primary focus, kept the

Soviet naval aviation operated Beriev MBR-2 flying boats in all fleets. Black Sea Fleet MBR-2s supported Zveno raids against Romania, and Northern Fleet MBR-2s raided coastal supply ships, helping to halt the German advance on Murmansk. (Nik Cornish at www.stavka.photos/)

HMS *Victorious* in 1941. Late in the year, the Royal Navy attempted to assist the Soviet defense of Murmansk with carrier airstrikes launched from *Victorious* and *Furious*, but 12 Albacores and four Fulmars were lost to enemy flak and fighters. (Lt R.G.G. Coote/Imperial War Museums via Getty Images)

Germans from allocating more forces to a theater that could have yielded significant strategic advantages at low cost.

The Axis and Soviet air arms in mid-campaign
The Luftwaffe

By late July 1941, it was clear that German plans for a brief six-week war against the USSR had been frustrated. Soviet ground and air forces had sustained huge losses, but they were battling for every foot of ground, and the Luftwaffe faced the challenge of maintaining air superiority and supporting multiple army groups fighting on a 2,500km-wide (1,553-mile) front. Like the Wehrmacht as a whole, the Luftwaffe was not prepared for sustained operations on this scale, and readiness began to suffer. Aircraft lost or damaged in combat along with accidents and maintenance problems reduced the number of aircraft available for flight operations. Operating from improvised airstrips led to accidents on takeoff and landing, and the motorized supply companies struggled to reach forward airfields over the primitive road network. The Luftwaffe's minimal forward maintenance capabilities meant that even minor damage or mechanical issues could ground aircraft. After the first week of fighting, Luftflotte 1, 2, and 4 reported that only 960 aircraft were operational. In six weeks, the serviceable fighter strength in all three Luftflotten fell from 657 to 363, and by the end of July, 760 aircraft had been lost to all causes, almost 30 percent of the strength of the force on June 22.

Luftwaffe strength July 5, 1941					
Type	LF 1	LF 2	LF 4	LF 5	Total
Fighter	144	279	286	18	727
Twin-engine fighter	–	78	–	10	88
Bomber	211	293	243	12	759
Stuka	–	164	113	37	314
Total	355	814	642	77	1,888

The Bf 109s continued to inflict heavy losses on their Soviet opponents, but the limited numbers of available fighters and vast frontage meant that many enemy sorties were not intercepted. The VVS would launch low-level strafing runs against German columns, often with fighters, and escape before any Bf 109s in the area could engage. Continuous defensive patrols over the troops were impossible, and with Luftwaffe flak units often pushed forward to aid the troops at the front, army marching columns had to rely on their own means for air defense and were ordered to fire all available weapons against any aircraft spotted overhead.

As the campaign progressed, German air commanders refined their interdiction techniques. The Luftwaffe found that striking villages and small cities to block road movement was much less useful in the Soviet Union than it had been in western Europe, as the buildings in the USSR were largely wooden and any damage was easily cleared or bypassed by Red Army columns using adjacent open fields. Strikes on crossing points over rivers and streams were more effective, especially when water levels were high. Attacking Soviet units moving behind the front also posed challenges, as the Red Army troops learned to take cover in forests and tree lines when spotted by reconnaissance aircraft, often eluding the following Luftwaffe strike aircraft. As a result, the German airman began to conduct armed reconnaissance, with dispersed formations of bombers and Stukas patrolling likely areas and immediately attacking enemy formations when caught in the open. To fully isolate the battlefield, the Luftwaffe relied on strikes against rail yards, track junctions, and bridges, as the Red Army relied on the railroads for logistics and long-distance troop movements. Luftwaffe planners worked closely with their ground force counterparts to identify major rail bridges for destruction, while others were reserved for seizure and use by the advancing panzer groups. The USSR had robust rail repair capabilities, however, which often frustrated German plans.

Friendly fire remained an issue during close-support operations, as pre-planned bomb lines rapidly became out-of-date due to the dynamic German advances. On occasion, Luftwaffe Stukas and bombers would abort strikes when aircrew were unable to differentiate between

A British Hurricane fighter operating in the Murmansk area. The British shipped Hurricane IIs to Murmansk along with a number of RAF pilots to familiarize the Soviets with the aircraft. (Nik Cornish at www.stavka.photos/)

enemy and friendly forces on the ground. Very lights, smoke, ground signal panels, swastika flags on tank decks, trucks, and wagons helped identify German forces, although the Soviets became adept at copying German recognition signals. With the VVS still vigorously launching strike operations, German ground units were on occasion hesitant to use recognition signals, as they could invite attacks by Soviet aircraft.

Luftwaffe personnel could be forced to fight on the ground as well as in the air. As support units displaced to forward airstrips or captured bases during fluid combat situations, the ground personnel often had to pick up small arms and defend against roving Soviet units or groups of partisans. With road communications difficult or insecure and the airbases far forward, Luftwaffe commanders relied heavily on light Fieseler Storch liaison aircraft to move between their units. The Flak Corps attached to Luftflotte 2 and 4 were often called forward to support ground units in addition to defending against Soviet aircraft. The high-velocity 88mm antiaircraft guns in particular proved to be superb tank-killers. By September 9, Army Group Center's antiaircraft forces reported the destruction of 369 enemy tanks as well as over 500 aircraft.

Exhausted pilots resting near their Bf 109 fighters. As the campaign in the USSR extended into summer and fall, the toll on Luftwaffe personnel and aircraft readiness steadily increased. (Nik Cornish at www.stavka.photos/)

The VVS

Luftwaffe intelligence had underestimated the strength of the VVS and was surprised by continued enemy resistance in the air. The USSR fielded almost 15,000 aircraft on June 22, with roughly two-thirds in the west and the remainder in military districts deeper in the Soviet Union. With the huge losses suffered during the first days of *Barbarossa*, the Stavka shifted aviation divisions and regiments from the rear area districts to restore the front, although units had to be retained in the Caucasus and Far East to guard against Turkey and Japan. Aircraft and aircrew from flight training schools were also sent to the front, and although the aircraft quality was poor, the reinforcements helped sustain force numbers.

Due to the poor road and rail networks available in 1941, the Luftwaffe was forced to rely heavily on its limited force of Ju 52 transport aircraft to fly critically needed fuel and ammunition to its forward airstrips. (Nik Cornish at www.stavka.photos/)

The VVS soon began to use its obsolete biplanes as light night bombers for harassment raids, a practice copied by the Luftwaffe later in the war. A third source of reinforcements was Soviet industry. The USSR produced 15,874 aircraft in 1941, two thirds after the invasion began, a remarkable achievement given the evacuation of Soviet industry by rail from the western Soviet Union to safer locations to the east. The USSR produced 2,329 aircraft in September, while just 987 left German factories in the same month.

On July 10, the VVS still had 2,516 combat aircraft on the frontlines: 1,532 fighters, 774 bombers, 128 ground attack, and 82 reconnaissance. Of the total, 1,900 were serviceable. By August, the Soviet air arm had been rebuilt to 3,700 aircraft at the front, although 1,100 were obsolescent aircraft from training schools. Although an increasing portion of the VVS was equipped with newly produced MiG-3s, Il-2s, and Pe-2s, the Luftwaffe's superior aircraft and pilots continued to inflict heavy attrition on the VVS, and new units sent to the front rapidly melted away in combat. In June, Moscow accepted a proposal from Stephen Suprun, a test pilot and a veteran of operations in China, to form regiments manned by test pilots to, as he said, "test the German aces." Suprun personally commanded the 401 OSNAZ (Special Purpose) Fighter Aviation Regiment equipped with MiG-3s. Both Suprun's 401 and the companion 402 OSNAZ IAPs proved capable at the front, and Suprun scored his first victory on June 27. While effective, like other VVS units the OSNAZ regiments took steady losses, with Suprun himself being killed in action on July 4. Many regiments were repeatedly withdrawn for rebuilding, often receiving new production aircraft, but staffed with new, hastily trained pilots and aircrew. Soviet air strength never regained the level it had had in early August 1941, and by October 1 was down to 1,716 including 948 fighters, 508 bombers, 180 ground-attack, and 80 reconnaissance aircraft.

To improve command and control of his embattled fronts, on July 10 Stalin and the Stavka authorized the formation of three *Glovkom* (high commands) to orchestrate the operations of its fronts and fleets on the three *Napravleniya* (Strategic Directions) at the front – the Northwestern, Western, and Southwestern. Each of the new commands had a senior VVS commander to coordinate aviation operations. On the Northwest Direction, for example, the VVS commander controlled the aviation forces of the Northern and Northwestern Fronts, the VVS Baltic Fleet, and the Leningrad PVO's 7 IAK (Fighter Corps). The headquarters themselves were, however, relatively small for their task, and two of the three commanders – Marshals Voroshilov and Budennyy – were incompetent Stalin cronies who failed at the front. By the beginning of Operation *Typhoon* in the late fall, Stalin and the Stavka had reverted to direct control and coordination of the various fronts and fleets by Moscow.

A German panzer commander overflown by a reconnaissance aircraft. Panzer groups relied heavily on Luftwaffe support for reconnaissance, to strike enemy centers of resistance, and to screen their flanks. (Nik Cornish at www.stavka.photos/)

Soviet forces			
Strategic Direction	Fronts and fleets controlled	Commander	VVS Commander
Northwest	Northern, Northwestern, Baltic Fleet	Marshal Kliment Voroshilov	General A.A. Novikov
Western	Western, Pinsk Flotilla	Marshal Semyon Timoshenko	Colonel N.F. Naumenko
Southwestern	Southwestern, Southern, Black Sea Fleet	Marshal Semyon Budennyy	General F. Ya. Falaleyev

The VVS streamlined its tables of organization and began to transition to two-regiment fighter, ground-attack, or bomber divisions rather than the large and complex mixed aviation divisions used at the beginning of the conflict. Reconnaissance regiments typically remained separate and subordinated to corps or frontal aviation headquarters. The prewar 62-strong fighter and frontal bomber and 40-strong heavy bomber regiments proved too cumbersome, and in July the tables of organization were reduced to 32 aircraft, with some fighter regiments equipped with new types operating only 22. The Stavka also realized the need to have a reserve of air assets available to rapidly reinforce critical sectors of the front and began to form the first *Rezervnaya Aviationnaya Gruppa* (Reserve Air Groups) on July 21. Six were formed in 1941, each containing 60 to 100 aircraft, and the practice continued through to the end of the war. Despite these improvements, aviation divisions assigned to each front continued to be split up and directly attached to subordinate armies, making it difficult for the VVS Front commander to concentrate his airpower. Only in early 1942 would Alexander Novikov, the new VVS Commander-in-Chief, form new air armies to control and centralize each front's airpower.

OPPOSITE THE COURSE OF AIR OPERATIONS, LATE AUGUST TO EARLY DECEMBER, 1941

The DBA long-range bomber force was reorganized in mid-August 1941. The prewar corps organization was intended to facilitate strategic bombing operations, but the force had lost 65 percent of its order of battle by August, and the repeated crises at the front had led to three-quarters of all DBA sorties being dedicated to support ground operations. As a result, the unwieldy bomber corps were disbanded and reformed on August 24 into eight new independent DBA divisions, with the surviving TB-3 four-engine bombers centralized in the 23 Heavy Bomber Aviation Division.

23 Heavy Bomber Aviation Division	
Unit	Operational area
40 DBAD	Northwest Direction
51 DBAD	Western Direction
22 DBAD	Southwestern Direction
42 DBAD	Southwestern Direction
50 DBAD	Southwestern Direction
52 DBAD	Southwestern Direction
23 TBAD	Centralized heavy bomber division
81 DBAD	Strategic operations – Berlin

The turn to the flanks: Leningrad and Kiev

The momentum of the Wehrmacht's advance waned in late July and August due to logistical shortfalls and the ongoing debate between Hitler and his high command about how to secure final victory. Kesselring viewed Moscow as the obvious next objective after the fall

A Soviet factory assembling Yak-1 fighters. Despite the evacuation of its industrial facilities thousands of miles to the east, the USSR still out-produced German aircraft production in 1941, and was able to dispatch fresh aircraft to the VVS to sustain air operations. By winter 1941–42, the VVS outnumbered its opponent on the frontline. (Getty Images)

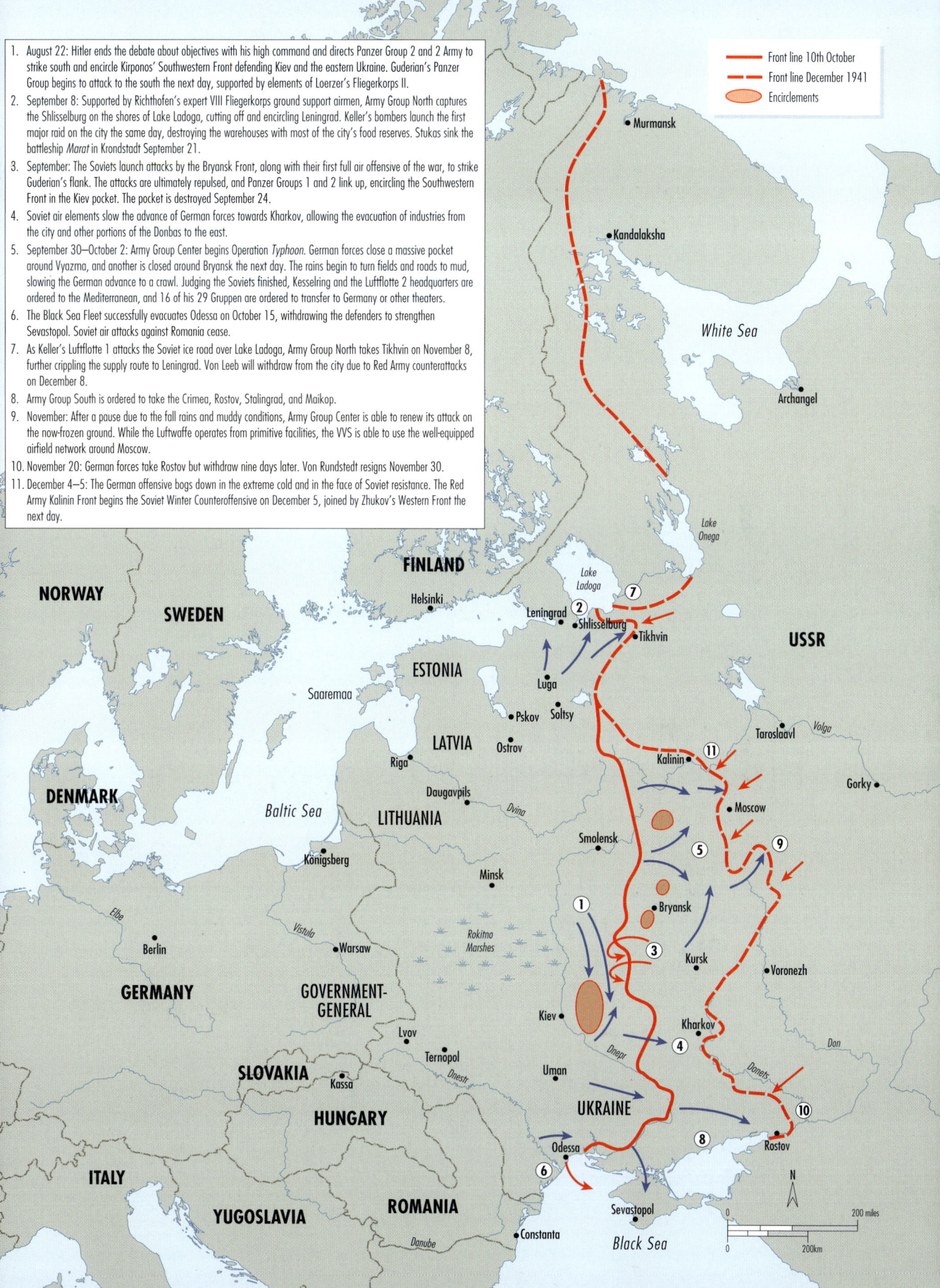

THE CAMPAIGN

Soviet pilots planning a mission near an I-153 Chaika. The VVS's command and control was less sophisticated than that of the Luftwaffe in 1941, with most aircraft lacking full radio sets and fewer radios at the regimental and divisional levels. (Getty Images)

of Smolensk, and Bock, Halder, and Guderian forcefully pushed for an advance on the Soviet capital. Hitler placed greater emphasis on securing Leningrad and the Ukraine, and on July 19 settled the issue with Directive Number 33. Hoth's panzers and Richthofen's Fliegerkorps VIII were ordered to reinforce the effort against Leningrad while Guderian's Panzer Group 2 struck south. In the center, the Luftwaffe was ordered to launch a bombing offensive against Moscow.

Luftflotte 2 on the defensive

The Soviets complicated German operations with their first major offensive of the war, aimed against Army Group Center and focused on seizing the Yelnya salient. With Richthofen's move north, Kesselring only had Loerzer's Fliegerkorps II to support the defense. Loerzer had lost his Stukas and his bombers were split between supporting the frontline and launching raids against Moscow. After a costly defensive battle, Army Group Center evacuated the Yelnya Salient on September 6. Soviet forces paid a high price for their victory, taking 218,000 casualties while the VVS lost 903 aircraft in the Yelnya sector between July and September.

Bombing Moscow

At the same time as Luftflotte 2 was struggling to support the hard-pressed infantrymen of Army Group Center, Kesselring's medium bomber force had to fulfill the Führer's orders to strike Moscow. Hitler had announced as early as July 8 his intention to have the Luftwaffe level both Moscow and Leningrad so that no inhabitants would be left for the Germans to supply during the winter. In late July, Hitler explicitly directed the Luftwaffe to attack the Soviet capital. At the time, the Luftwaffe had a total of only 673 twin-engine bombers on the entire Eastern Front, including 411 Ju 88s, 215 He 111s, and 47 Do 17s. For the attack on Moscow, Göring had to cobble together a force including both Luftflotte 2's KG 3 and KG 53, reinforced by 119 bombers transferred from France, the Mediterranean, and Norway.

Luftwaffe reinforcements for Luftflotte 2's attack on Moscow, July, 1941				
Unit	Bomber type	Total	Operational	Notes
KG 4 "General Wever"	He 111	58	45	Specialized mine-laying unit
III./KG 26	He 111	29	21	Specialized unit for anti-shipping operations
KGr 100 "Wiking"	He 111	12	12	Pathfinders
I./KG 28	He 111	20	14	Torpedo-bomber group from Norway

The Luftwaffe would face the searchlights, barrage balloons, and antiaircraft guns of the Moskovskaya Zona PVO, along with the fighters of the PVO's 6 IAK (Fighter Aviation Corps). The 6 IAK controlled 29 regiments with 495 fighters, half of them modern MiG-3s, Yak-1s, and LaGG-3s. The PVO zone also had RUS-2 radars, but there was no integrated air defense system, so the fighters operating against the bombers at night typically relied on searchlights to track and engage their targets.

Moscow air defense district, July, 1941	
Antiaircraft guns	1,044
Antiaircraft machine guns	336
I-16 fighters	170
I-153 fighters	70
LaGG-3 fighters	37
Yak-1 fighters	91
MiG-3 fighters	127

Kesselring was able to mount three consecutive raids on Moscow, each of more than 100 bombers. The offensive, dubbed Operation *Clara Zetkin* after the founder of the German Communist Party, began on the night of July 21/22. As the Bf 109s were unable to escort the bombers to Moscow and back, the raids were conducted during the hours of darkness. Kesselring sent 195 bombers against a variety of targets including the Kremlin, railroad stations, factories, and the power station, and 127 were able to reach and deliver their bombloads over the city. The Soviet defenders were alerted to the raids due to British Ultra intercepts, so the bombers were met by heavy antiaircraft fire and 170 fighter sorties. KGr 100 pathfinders dropped incendiaries to mark the target zone, and the following waves of He 111s, Ju 88s, and Do 17s delivered 104 tons of high explosives and 46,000 incendiaries from altitudes of 2,000–4,000m (6,561ft–13,123ft). Moscow suffered 792 casualties, 150 of them fatal, but the one bomb to hit the Kremlin palace did not detonate. Soviet fighters claimed to have downed eight bombers and the antiaircraft gunners four, but while several bombers were damaged, only one Do 17 and one He 111 were shot down and another He 111 and a Ju 88 destroyed while crash-landing.

Reconnaissance photos showed little damage to Moscow, so the next night the Luftwaffe returned with 115 bombers. The raid delivered 98 tons of high explosives and 34,000 incendiaries, and this time the bombers flew at higher altitudes to avoid Soviet antiaircraft fire. The bombs damaged 63 factory buildings, 96 houses, and the Moscow power plant. Several of KG 53's bombs struck Red Square, with one detonating in front of Lenin's Mausoleum, but the Kremlin was not hit. One He 111 from KG 28 was damaged by antiaircraft fire and destroyed during an emergency landing, although the crew survived. The next night, the Luftwaffe was able to return with 125 bombers, delivering an additional 140 tons of bombs. The third attack was launched through heavy cloud cover, minimizing the effectiveness of antiaircraft fire, and only one He 111 was damaged.

A Dornier Do 17 delivering its bombs. 47 Do 17s were operational on the Eastern Front during late July and joined in the Luftwaffe raids on Moscow. The 1941 campaign was the swan song for the bomber, which was removed from active service and replaced by Ju 88s. (Nik Cornish at www.stavka.photos/)

The Luftwaffe had conducted 435 sorties against the capital over three nights with only minor losses, but the damage to Moscow was limited, and the demand for bomber support at the front led Luftflotte 2 to switch to a program of smaller-scale raids. The Luftwaffe managed a total of 87 by April 5, 1942, and in addition to the three initial raids, six involved 50 bombers apiece, 19 consisted of 19 to 40, and 59 were carried out by three to ten aircraft. From July 22 to August 22, German bombs had injured 3,513 and killed 736 civilians, but Soviet sources estimated that only three percent of the city was damaged by the attacks. PVO fighters flew 1,015 night intercept sorties in July alone, but they had difficulties finding and engaging the bombers. As the pilots had little training for night operations, 36 fighters were lost in landing accidents. The Soviets publicized extensively their exaggerated claims of heavy losses inflicted on the bombers for morale purposes. Lieutenant Viktor Talalikhin's ramming of an He 111 on the night of August 5, the first night taran of the war, received particular attention both in the USSR and in the West.

Bombing Berlin

The Soviets determined to launch retaliatory raids against the German capital, using bases on the Baltic Islands to reach the target. The Baltic Fleet's 8 Bomber Division was given the mission, and 20 DB-3Ts from its 1 MTAP (Mine and Torpedo) and 57 BAP (Bomber Aviation) Regiments flew to Saaremaa Island on August 4. Five DB-3s flew a reconnaissance flight the next day, and on August 7, 15 bombers took off to make the 1,000km (621-mile) flight to Berlin. Five bombers arrived over the German capital, initially meeting no antiaircraft fire as they approached from an unusual direction and were mistaken for friendly aircraft. The next night, 12 DB-3s made the run, dropping 72 100kg (220lb) FAB-100 high-explosive bombs and 2,500 propaganda leaflets. One aircraft was shot down by German flak.

A PVO 85mm antiaircraft gun in front of St Isaacs' Cathedral in Leningrad. Both Leningrad and Moscow were heavily defended by Soviet Homeland Air Defense PVO forces, including antiaircraft artillery and machine guns, searchlights, and barrage balloons. The 6 PVO IAK (Fighter Aviation Corps) patrolled over the capital, and the 7 IAK defended Leningrad. (From the fonds of the RGAKFD in Krasnogorsk via Stavka)

The raids aroused great enthusiasm in the Soviet Union, and the 81 DBA Division was sent to join the Baltic Fleet bombers with its TB-7/Pe-8s, the most modern bombers in the Soviet arsenal, along with twin-engine Yermolayev Yer-2s. In the event, the TB-7's diesel engines proved unreliable, and during their first mission, on August 10, five TB-7s and two Yer-2s were lost and two Yer-2s damaged due to crashes on takeoff or mechanical failures, and only four aircraft reached the city. The next night, eight DB-3s from DBA and VVS Baltic Fleet bombed Berlin and the commander of 1 Mine and Torpedo Regiment and four of the pilots were made Heroes of the Soviet Union the next day. The critical situation on the front in Estonia forced the 1 MTAP to be diverted for operations against von Leeb's troops, so on the night of August 18, only the DBA flew, with five DB-3s reaching Berlin. Stalin was closely monitoring the operation, and ordered heavier bombs be used to compensate for the small number of aircraft able to reach Berlin.

The DB-3s had 1,000kg (2,204lb) FAB-1000s and 500kg (1,102lb) FAB-500s mounted on eternal racks on August 19, causing two to crash on takeoff. German landings on the Baltic Islands on September 9 halted the raids. Overall, the Soviets launched nine missions with a total of 54 bombers against Berlin from Saaremaa, with 20 lost to accidents or enemy action. The RAF renewed its attacks against the German capital during this period, with 70 British bombers striking Berlin on August 13 and 200 on September 7.

The attack on Leningrad

In early August, Richthofen arrived from Army Group Center to support von Leeb's assault against Leningrad. Fliegerkorps VIII brought the Stukas of StG 1 and StG 2 along with the close-support Bf 109s and Hs 123s of LG 2, Do 17 bombers in KGs 2 and 3, and Bf 109s in JGs 27 and 53. The renewed Army Group North offensive kicked off on August 8, with Foerster's Fliegerkorps I supporting Panzer Group 4 while Richthofen's Fliegerkorps VIII operated on the right flank with the 16 Army. Novikov's defending airmen were hard-pressed, as 142 of his 560 available aircraft were diverted to oppose a Finnish offensive in Karelia that was threatening Leningrad from the north.

On August 12, the Red Army launched a counterattack at Staraya Russa aiming to pin the 16 Army's 10 Corps against Lake Ilmen. The counterattack caused alarm at Army Group North headquarters, and one of Panzer Group 4's corps was pulled from the main attack to the north. Richthofen brought his ruthless energy, expertise in close-air support, and the Fliegerkorps VIII's excellent communication network to bear, throwing in all available aircraft to destroy the attackers. His airmen flew 4,742 sorties in 12 days of intense activity, dropping more than 3,300 tons of bombs. The effort cost Richthofen 27 aircraft destroyed and 143

A Soviet naval aviator from the 1 MTAP of the Baltic Fleet holds up a FAB-50 50kg (110lb) bomb with the message "a gift for Hitler" for a publicity photo. While small in scale, the raids on Berlin were heavily publicized in the USSR, and as a morale-raising exercise paralleled the 1942 US Doolittle raid on Tokyo. (Courtesy of the Central Museum of the Armed Forces, Moscow via Stavka)

Air raid wardens on the alert in Leningrad. Although the Soviets had RUS-2 radars in the Moscow area, these were not linked in any integrated air defense network, and both Moscow and Leningrad relied on spotter reports, sound-ranging, and searchlights to identify aerial attackers. (Nik Cornish at www.stavka.photos/)

damaged. In early September, Leeb renewed the attack to isolate Leningrad. Luftflotte 1 brought 468 operational aircraft to support the offensive, outnumbering Novikov's remaining 163. On September 8, Army Group North forces with strong support from Fliegerkorps VIII seized Shlisselburg on the southern shore of Lake Ladoga, cutting off the city. The Red Army launched a series of attacks to restore land communications with Leningrad, placing intense pressure on Army Group North, and to meet the desperate need for more infantry to hold the siege lines, the Luftwaffe organized an air bridge to fly in emergency reinforcements. Over 50 Ju 52s delivered the I. and III. Battalions of the 7th Fliegerdivision's Paratroop Regiment 1 and the II Battalion of the Luftlande-Sturmregiment to the battlefront. Some 12 Ju 52s towed gliders to supply the defending troops with mines.

Luftflotte 1 began sustained raids on Leningrad the day Shlisselburg was captured. Twenty-seven Ju 88s delivered incendiary bombers that started 183 fires, destroying the Badayevo warehouses with most of the city's food reserves. The Luftwaffe continued to bomb the city throughout the month, with most raids conducted at night due to the effective Soviet antiaircraft fire and the fighters of the 7 PVO Fighter Aviation Corps, which had received seven regiments as reinforcements. In total, the Luftwaffe would drop roughly 1,500 tons of high-explosive bombs on the city between September and December, 79 percent of the raids that would be launched against Leningrad throughout the entire war.

Loehr's *Fliegerführer Ostsee* (Air Leader Baltic) had been effective over the Baltic, flying 1,175 sorties by August, laying extensive minefields that confined the Soviet Baltic Fleet to the waters around Kronstadt, and supporting the amphibious operations against the Baltic Islands in September with a further 1,524 sorties. Although confined to Kronstadt, the Soviet battleships were able to support Leningrad's defenders with long-range gunfire and the

PVO barrage balloons in Leningrad. Both Moscow and Leningrad PVO forces used barrage balloons to drive Luftwaffe bombers to operate at higher altitudes. (From the fonds of the RGAKFD in Krasnogorsk via Stavka)

Luftwaffe mounted a series of strikes against the port. The 23,600-ton battleship *Marat* was a primary target and it was damaged on September 16 by a 500kg (1,102lb) bomb delivered by an StG 2 Stuka. The Stukas returned on September 23 with more capable 1,000kg (2,204lb) armor-piercing bombs and scored several hits before a final bomb delivered by Stuka ace Hans-Ulrich Rudel caused a massive explosion. The *Marat* sank to the bottom of the shallow harbor, although its rear turrets were above the waterline and still able to fire. The *M-74* submarine, destroyer leader *Minsk*, and destroyer *Steregushchiy* were sunk in the same raid, and the battleship *Oktyabrskaya Revolutsiya* and two additional destroyers were damaged, but the Baltic Fleet was still able to provide the defenders of the city with significant gunfire support. On October 27, Wild's *Fliegerführer Ostsee* formation was disbanded, with the staff dispatched to coordinate operations in the Crimea and the aircraft sent to the Mediterranean, Norway, and France.

Hitler had ordered Leningrad destroyed by starvation, and, in late September, Panzer Group 4 and Richthofen's Fliegerkorps VIII were transferred back to the center for the assault on Moscow, along with the Ju 88s of Luftflotte 1's KG 76. The last daylight bombing raid on Leningrad took place on September 29, followed by raids on the Soviet supply lines across Lake Ladoga and night raids on the city. The Soviets also began to concentrate available resources for the defense of Moscow, and the VVS elements defending Leningrad received only 450 replacement aircraft despite the loss of 1,283 in September. On September 22, the VVS defenders had 191 aircraft, and the PVO fighter force had been reduced from 445 pilots on July 1 to 88 on October 1.

Kiev, Kharkov, and the Donbas

Soviet forces fell back to the Dnieper after the destruction of the Uman pocket by Army Group South on August 8. Two weeks later, Guderian's Panzer Group 2 began its attack south, threatening Kirponos's Southern Front from the rear. Fliegerkorps II supported the attack with KG 3 and KG 53 striking Soviet rail communications, while JG 51 Bf 109s and SKG 210 Bf 110s ranged ahead of the panzer columns seeking targets. Guderian's thrust to the south exposed a long left flank, and Stalin ordered General Andrey Yeremenko's

LENINGRAD 5
Pushkin Aerodrome

Soviet bomber raids on Berlin, August–September, 1941

10

EVENTS

1. On July 19, Hitler orders the Luftwaffe to launch an air campaign to destroy Moscow. Assembling a force of bombers from as far away as France and the Mediterranean, Luftflotte 2 commander Kesselring launches three raids, each of over 100 bombers, during the nights of July 21–25, and a series of smaller raids continues into 1942.

2. Naval Air Force Commander General Semyon Zhavaronokov assembles a force to retaliate with strikes on Berlin. To reach the German capital, the most capable crews and 20 DB-3Ts from the Baltic Fleet's 8th Bomber Aviation Division's 1 MTAP (Mine and Torpedo Aviation Regiment) and 57 BAP (Bomber Aviation Regiment) deploy to Kagul airfield on the island of Saaremaa.

3. Five bomber crews fly a reconnaissance mission to the Berlin area on August 4. Ten DB-3Ts bomb the port of Ventspils on the night of August 5–6.

4. On the night of August 7–8, 1 MTAP Commander Colonel Yevgeniy Preobrazhenskiy leads three groups totaling 15 DB-3Ts on the first raid on Berlin. As the bombers are approaching from an unusual direction, they are initially identified as friendly aircraft, and five drop 30 FAB-100 bombs over the city center, with the other groups dropping their bombs on the outskirts. 12 bombers deliver 72 FAB-100s and 2,500 propaganda leaflets the next night, and one bomber is shot down by German flak.

5. News of the raids is enthusiastically received by the Soviet population, and Long-Range Aviation (DBA) is ordered to reinforce the operation. The 1 BAK's 22 and 200 regiments send DB-3s and DB-3Fs to Aste airfield on Saaremaa, and the 81 Long-Range Bomber Aviation Division (DBAD) deploys to Pushkin Aerodrome near Leningrad. The 81 DBAD is newly formed, but it has some of the most experienced DBA crews and is equipped with several of the new TB-7/Pe-8 four-engine bombers.

6. The TB-7's diesel engines prove unreliable and the 81 DBAD's first attempt to raid Berlin ends in disaster. Five TB-7s and two Yer-2 bombers crash on take off or during the operation, and one TB-7 is engaged in error over the Baltic Sea by a naval aviation I-16. The 81 DBAD commander is relieved due to the fiasco.

7. On the night of August 11–12, eight DBA and naval aviation DB-3s renew the attack on Berlin, dropping six FAB-250s, 26 FAB-100Ts, 48 FAB-50s, and over 100,000 propaganda leaflets. Four bombers divert to bomb Libau, and another bombs Kohlberg.

8. Stalin orders that heavier bombs be used to compensate for the small number of bombers, but the heavy loads and short runways cause two DB-3s to crash while taking off from Aste on August 19 and two on August 20.

9. On September 6, ZG 26 Bf 110s raid Kagul, destroying six of 1 MTAP's DB-3Ts.

10. On September 8, German forces begin Operation *Beowulf*, an amphibious operation against Saaremaa, causing the Soviets to evacuate the airfields.

The Soviets launched nine raids on Berlin with a total of 54 aircraft, and 20 were lost to enemy action or technical failures. The raids were highly publicized in the USSR, and Preobrazhenskiy of the 1 MTAP and four of his pilots were appointed Heroes of the Soviet Union.

A ZPU 4M PVO machine gun. Despite its strong air defenses, on September 8, Leningrad suffered perhaps the most deadly loss of the 1941 war when the East Warehouses where the city's food supply was kept were destroyed by fires started by a Luftwaffe bomber raid. (TASS)

newly formed Bryansk Front into the attack. The Stavka reinforced the Front's VVS forces, commanded by General Fyodor Plynin, with additional aviation regiments from the Transcaucasus Front, PVO, training units, Naval Aviation, and the 1 Reserve Air Group. Two DBA bomber divisions, the 42 and 52, were attached in support. The force of 464 aircraft would conduct a full "air offensive," the first such VVS operation of the war, and a prototype for what would become the standard application of VVS airpower in 1943–45.

The Luftwaffe soon felt the impact from the concentrated attack, and for the first time in the war, Il-2s were used in appreciable numbers. VVS fighters mounted six to seven sorties a day and the SBs, Pe-2s, and Il-2s three to four. The veteran pilots of JG 51 were shifted to cover Guderian's columns, reporting 34 Soviet aircraft shot down for the loss of only two on August 30, and Göring personally directed that Stukas and Bf 110s of StG 1 and SKG 210 be sent to protect Guderian's flank. The Luftwaffe Bf 109s steadily wore down their opponents and Plynin's force was rapidly reduced to 103 operational aircraft. On September 8, the same day JG 51 claimed its 2,000th victory of the war, the Bryansk Front began to withdraw to the east.

The intense fighting for Guderian's flank cost the Luftwaffe one of its leading aces, Captain Hermann-Friedrich Joppien, shot down by a Yak-1 from the 201 Fighter Aviation Regiment immediately after scoring his 70th victory. The fighting also claimed the life of one of the first VVS woman pilots, Lieutenant Yekaterine Zelyenko, who had flown eight sorties during the Winter War with Finland. Flying an Su-2 of 135 BAP, Zelyenko was killed attempting to ram a Bf 109 after her three-ship Vic was bounced by German fighters. Zelyenko was made a posthumous Hero of the Soviet Union by Mikhail Gorbachev on May 5, 1990.

As Guderian battled south, Kleist's Panzer Group 1 broke out of its bridgehead over the Dnieper and advanced to the north with heavy fighter cover and Stuka sorties clearing the way. Fliegerkorps V flew 156 bomber, 122 fighter, and 14 reconnaissance sorties on September 12, and its pilots claimed 100 victories during the first 13 days of the month. Red Army troops reported they could not move in the open due to the intense Luftwaffe air attacks. Although Germany's Romanian allies were fully engaged in the siege of Odessa, Luftflotte 4 was now augmented by squadrons from Slovakia and Hungary. The newly arrived 22nd Gruppo Caccia from Italy with 51 MC-200 S Saetta single-engine fighters also joined the offensive, and the Italian airmen shot down six SBs and one I-16 for no loss in their first combat on the Eastern Front on August 27.

On September 16, Guderian's and Kleist's leading panzer divisions met, encircling Kirponos's Southwestern Front in a huge pocket. Loehr temporarily grounded his medium bombers due to the shortage of fuel at his forward airstrips, concentrating on keeping

Ernst Rudel and a second Ju 87 crew score the hits on the *Marat* at Kronstadt that sink the battleship, September 23, 1941. Despite the successful Stuka attacks, Baltic Fleet units were still able to support Leningrad's defenders with naval gunfire throughout the winter. (Nik Cornish at www.stavka.photos/)

Luftflotte 4's Stukas in the air. The Ju 87s were able to inflict heavy losses on the pinned troops, destroying 920 vehicles on one day alone. Kiev fell on September 19 and the pocket collapsed seven days later with the loss of 42 Red Army divisions and over 440,000 troops. Kirponos was killed and the VVS Southwestern Front commander, General Fyodor Astakhov, was listed as missing, although he was able to evade capture and return to Soviet lines in November.

With the collapse of Soviet defenses, Army Group South began to exploit with widely separated advances into the Crimea, towards Rostov, and directly east towards Kharkov

Striking back at Berlin (overleaf)

The Soviets were determined to retaliate for the Luftwaffe's raids on Moscow, but they needed bases to be able to reach Berlin. Supplies of ammunition and aviation fuel were shipped by small barges through German minefields to prepare bases on the Moonsund Archipelago in the Baltic for bomber operations. When the naval aviation DB-3Ts began to arrive during the first days of August, they were dispersed and camouflaged to avoid alerting the Luftwaffe.

On August 6, five Soviet bombers flew a successful reconnaissance sortie from the now-ready airfield on Osel Island (present-day Saaremaa), and 15 bombers from the Red Banner Fleet's 1 Mine-Torpedo Aviation Regiment took off the next day. The flight covered almost 1,000km (621 miles), mostly over the Baltic Sea and turning into the coast around Stettin. Five of the DB-3Ts delivered their loads over Berlin, with the other two groups of five each bombing the suburbs and Stettin. The RAF had not attacked the capital since June, and the Soviet bombers were initially assumed to be friendly. Berlin's searchlight and antiaircraft defenses were activated as the bombs began to hit. All the bombers returned safely, having delivered 30 100kg (220lb) high-explosive bombs over the city center, killing six civilians and injuring 17. The leaflets that followed the bombs proved the attackers were Soviet, but due to German prejudice, newspapers the next day reported the raid was by RAF bombers, and claimed six were shot down.

All 12 of the DB-3Ts launched on night of August 8–9 reached Berlin, dropping 72 100kg (220lb) FAB-100 bombs and 2,500 propaganda leaflets, with one bomber lost to enemy flak. The Soviets added DBA bombers to the effort and continued operations against Berlin until German attacks on the Baltic Islands forced a halt in early September. The nine raids on Berlin employed a total of 54 bombers, 20 of them lost to accidents or enemy action. The damage inflicted on Berlin was small, but like the US Doolittle raid on Tokyo ten months later, raised the morale of the Soviet populace. The RAF renewed operations against Berlin during the same period, with 70 bombers on the night of August 13 and almost 200 on the night of September 7.

and the Donbas industrial region. Soviet forces were shattered by the losses at Kiev and the VVS assembled what aviation resources were available to cover the ongoing evacuation of industries from Kharkov and the Donbas. The 1 Reserve Air Group and 16 and 19 SADs in the area only had 15 Il-2s and numbers of R-Z biplanes, now employed as light night bombers, but they were able to slow the advance of German infantry towards Kharkov to a crawl. The Luftwaffe had not yet established air cover over the infantry, and the obsolete I-153 fighter bombers proved particularly effective at striking the long horse-drawn artillery and transport columns.

The Luftwaffe was thinly stretched, with Luftflotte 4's bombers scattered to support operations in Odessa, the Crimea, and the Black Sea, and JG 51 and JG 53 with only 12 serviceable Bf 109s each. Loehr sent KG 55 to halt the evacuation of industrial equipment from the area. The 111s flew free-hunting raids to destroy the railroad infrastruture, leading the Soviets to shift rail operations to the night or periods of poor weather, and to pre-position rail repair units and equipment along the network. German forces ultimately reached Kharkov on October 24, but found only empty factory buildings. The majority of Kharkov's industrial resources, including T-34 tank and aircraft plants, along with Stalino's 223 large and 54 small or medium factories, had been successfully evacuated to the Urals.

An He 111 on a bombing run. He 111 bombers were some of the Luftwaffe's most capable assets for strikes against Red Army lines of communications, in particular rail yards. (Nik Cornish WH 931)

Operation *Typhoon*

By September 30, Axis forces had advanced 800km (497 miles) into the USSR and inflicted huge losses on Soviet ground and air forces, but *Barbarossa*'s ultimate goal – the destruction of Stalin's regime – remained unfulfilled. Hitler now turned to Moscow, assessing that the importance of the capital would lead the Soviets to mass their remaining forces for its defense. Panzer Group 4 was transferred to Army Group Center for the offensive, and Guderian would return from the Kiev operation, attacking to the northeast. Army Groups North and South were to continue their advances, von Leeb to establish contact with Finnish forces, while to the south Rundstedt was given ambitious objectives including the seizure of the Crimea, Rostov, and the oilfields of the Caucasus.

Kesselring had about 550 operational aircraft as Operation *Typhoon* began. Richthofen's Fliegerkorps VIII returned from Army Group North to join Fliegerkorps II in the center, although its high-intensity operations to the north left it little time for refurbishment. Kesselring's Luftflotte 2 was further reinforced by two JG 53 Gruppen transferred from Luftflotte 4 as well as a JG 52 Gruppe from western Europe. A Spanish squadron, Escuadrilla Azul *(Blue Squadron)*, designated by the Luftwaffe as 15.(Span)/JG 27, joined the attack with Bf 109 E-7s flown by Spanish Civil War veterans. Kesselring's I Flak Corps was assigned to support Guderian along with the 2 and 4 Armies to the south, and Loehr's II Flak Corps was transferred north and assigned to support the operations of Panzer Group 4. The three opposing Soviet fronts controlled 568 aircraft, with 373 serviceable. Also available to support Soviet defenses were the 423 fighters, 343 of them serviceable, of the Moscow PVO's 6 Fighter Corps, and 368 DBA bombers.

Soviet force structure October 2, 1941, Moscow			
Front	Commander	VVS Commander	Aircraft
Western	General Ivan Konev	General Fyodor Michugin	272
Reserve	Marshal Semyon Budennyy	General Yevgeniy Nikolayenko	126
Bryansk	General Andrey Yeremenko	General Fyodor Polynin	170

Soviet Aviation Forces at the beginning of Operation *Typhoon*				
Aircraft type	Frontal aviation	Long-range aviation	PVO fighter aviation	Total
Bomber	210	368	–	578
Fighter	285	–	423	708
Shturmovik	36	–	–	36
Recon	37	–	9	46
Total	568	368	432	1,368

Guderian's panzers began *Typhoon* with their attack from the south on September 30. Fog limited air support on the first day, but concentrated attacks by StG 77's Stukas helped the panzers break through on October 1. The next day, the rest of Army Group Center joined the offensive and Luftflotte 2 flew a total of 1,387 sorties, including a raid by 18 KG 77 Ju 88s that disabled the Western Front's headquarters. Kesselring reported 984 total sorties and claimed 679 Soviet vehicles destroyed on October 3. Richthofen's expert close-support Fliegerkorps kept a concentrated aerial strike force over the 9 Army and Panzer Group 3 on the northern wing of the offensive, with his aircraft averaging four sorties on October 2, and the ground-attack Bf 109s and Hs 123s managing to fly six. Loerzer's Fliegerkorps II supported the operations of Guderian's Panzer Group 2 and the accompanying 2 Army on the southern wing with a mix of direct support and deeper strike missions, including attacks on Moscow area airfields. Orel was captured and its airfield used as a forward base for Stukas and Bf 109s, and a hub for flying in supplies.

Stuka crewmen readying for a mission. During the fighting to destroy the Kiev pocket, Luftflotte 4 grounded its other aircraft to prioritize the limited supply of fuel for its force of Ju 87 Stukas. (Nik Cornish at www.stavka.photos/)

The rapid panzer advances and fluid situation led to friendly fire attacks from roving Luftwaffe aircraft despite the ground forces' use of recognition signals. The Bf 109s had trouble covering the fast-advancing panzer and motorized divisions, and the Soviets were able to launch repeated low-level fighter strafing runs and Il-2 rocket and cannon attacks. To be able to cover the panzers, the Luftwaffe began leapfrogging their fighters to advanced airfields and flying in support

OPPOSITE THE STRUCTURAL EVOLUTION OF GERMAN FORCES DURING *BARBAROSSA*, AUGUST TO DECEMBER, 1941

In August 1941, Richthofen's Fliegerkorps VIII formation was operating with Army Group North to support the assault on Leningrad. Kesselring's Luftflotte 2 was only left with Loerzer's Fliegerkorps II and was hard-pressed to resist the Soviet offensive on Yelnya, bomb Moscow, and support the advance of the 2 Army and Guderian's Panzer Group 2 to the south to encircle the Soviet Southwestern Front defending Kiev and the line of the Dnieper. Loehr's V and Fliegerkorps IV were supporting the attack of Army Group South ground forces towards Kiev and across the Dnieper, with few resources left to assist Romanian forces besieging Odessa or for maritime operations over the Black Sea.

By October 10, Luftflotte 2 was heavily strengthened for Operation *Typhoon*, the final assault on Moscow, with over half of the total Gruppen on the Eastern Front. Army Group North was advancing towards Tikhvin and keeping pressure on Leningrad by bombing and shelling the city and its supply lines over Lake Ladoga. Luftflotte 4 was unable to support its many missions – taking the Crimea, Sevastopol, the Donbas, Rostov, and the Caucasus oilfields – with the Gruppen remaining with its Fliegerkorps V and IV.

By December 20, Luftwaffe forces had been reduced by half due to Berlin's view that the war in the east was won. Luftflotte 1's Air Commander Baltic maritime formation was disbanded on October 27 and its aircraft ordered to other theaters. Luftflotte 2's and Fliegerkorps II's headquarters were withdrawn to prepare for operations against Malta, and Greim's Fliegerkorps V headquarters was ordered to Brussels to establish a new mine-laying corps. By this time, over half of the Gruppen assigned to support Army Group Center's assault on Moscow had been ordered to other theaters or to Germany for rebuilding.

A Ju 87 Stuka operating from an unimproved, and muddy, airstrip. The onset of the rainy season in October, along with continuing resistance from the Red Army and VVS, slowed the advance of Army Group Center against Moscow to a crawl. (Nik Cornish at www.stavka.photos/)

personnel and equipment by Ju 52, even when the area was not fully secure. The Ju 52s also supported the ground advance, flying in fuel to advanced airstrips to keep the panzer divisions moving.

The Stavka dispatched the 6 RAG to reinforce the hard-pressed Bryansk Front as Guderian drove rapidly to the northeast, and DBA TB-3s and GVF (Civil Aviation) PS-84s – Soviet-produced versions of the C-47 – flew 5,500 troops and 13 tons of ammunition to help block his advance. Guderian described the VVS as "lively" due to the continuous attacks on his divisions, and at one point Soviet bombs shattered the windows and sent glass flying in a building housing a corps headquarters he was visiting. Despite the Soviet reinforcements,

German forces structural evolution: *Barbarossa*, August – December, 1941

These diagrams show the evolution of the Luftwaffe force structure during the last months of Operation *Barbarossa*.
The number next to the Luftflotte symbol indicates the total number of Gruppen (full strength 30 aircraft) in that formation at that time.
Next to the Fliegerkorps symbol, three numbers indicate the numbers of bomber/Stuka, ground attack or Zerstörer/Bf 109 Gruppe.

August 5, 1941

- 1 LF (XXXX): **23**
  - I FK (XXX): 8/2/4
  - Baltic
  - VIII FK (XXX): 2/5/2
- 2 LF (XXXX): **10**
  - II FK (XXX): 4/2/4
- 4 LF (XXXX): **20**
  - V FK (XXX): 5/3/5
  - IV FK (XXX): 5/0/2

Total Gruppen: 53
Force: 24/12/17

October 10, 1941

- 1 LF (XXXX): **9**
  - I FK (XXX): 6/0/3
  - Baltic
- 2 LF (XXXX): **30**
  - VIII FK (XXX): 5/4/3
  - VIII FK (XXX): 7/5/6
- 4 LF (XXXX): **13**
  - V FK (XXX): 4/0/1
  - IV FK (XXX): 4/0/4

Total Gruppen: 52
Force: 26/9/17

December 20, 1941

- 1 LF (XXXX): **6**
  - I FK (XXX): 3/0/3
- 2 LF (XXXX): **6**
  - I FK (XXX): 2/2/2
- 4 LF (XXXX): **9**
  - IV FK (XXX): 5/2/2

Total Gruppen: 21
Force: 10/4/7

Luftflotte 2 still outflew the VVS, flying 958 sorties on October 4 to the VVS's 328 and reporting 450 Soviet vehicles destroyed. A counterattack by the Bryansk Front was met with 152 Stuka and 259 bomber sorties, while 202 Stukas and 188 medium bomber sorties struck the front's supply columns.

On October 5, a Pe-2 reconnaissance mission reported a column from Panzer Group 4 deep behind the Soviet frontline threatening to link up with divisions from Panzer Group 3. The Stavka ordered the commander of the Moscow District Air Force who forwarded the report to be interrogated by the NKVD for panic mongering, but the sighting was soon confirmed. The panzers linked up on October 7, encircling a massive pocket around Vyazma. The commander of the 50 Army in the pocket, General-Mayor Mikhail Petrov, was badly wounded by air attack and died three days later. To the south, the 2 Army and Guderian's Panzer Group 2 encircled the bulk of the Bryansk Front. On October 12, Luftflotte 2 launched 350 sorties, and the commander of the Bryansk Front, General Andrey Yeremenko, was wounded by bomb shrapnel and flown out of pocket.

The Vyazma pocket collapsed on October 13, and the Bryansk seven days later. The last, and largest, encirclement operation of *Barbarossa* led to the capture of 673,000 prisoners, 1,277 tanks, and 4,378 artillery pieces. A 500km-wide (310-mile) gap was torn in the Soviet lines in front of Moscow, and the massive haul of prisoners at Bryansk and Vyazma

Wounded Luftwaffe prisoners of war. Although Germany lost far fewer aircraft than the Soviets, the steady attrition of veteran pilots and aircrew from enemy action and accidents reduced the overall quality of the force and led Luftwaffe leadership to begin shortening the training programs for new pilots in 1942. (TASS)

convinced Hitler and the German high command that the war in the east was won. The Luftwaffe was accordingly directed to prepare to transfer units to other fronts or back to Germany for recuperation while planning began for a modestly sized Luftgau Moskau (Air District Moscow) to patrol the area after the fall of the capital. The headquarters of Luftflotte 2 and Fliegerkorps II were ordered to deploy to the Mediterranean and about one half of Kesselring's overall strength, the equivalent of 16 Gruppen, began to leave the front. On October 11, Werner Mölders arrived on an inspection visit to a JG 27 airfield and witnessed the Bf 109s scramble and shoot down three attacking Il-2s and one MiG-3. Mölders was gratified by the successful action, but he had just witnessed the unit's last victories in the USSR in 1941, and the fighters departed for Germany a few days later. On November 11, Kesselring and his Luftflotte 2 headquarters, along with Fliegerkorps II HQ, departed for the Mediterranean to begin operations against Malta. Richthofen's Fliegerkorps VIII was left behind with roughly 13 Gruppen to provide a measure of close-air support for Army Group Center.

Despite the drawdown and the need to launch the final drive on Moscow, the Luftwaffe continued small-scale bombing raids against the Soviet capital and other industrial targets. Luftflotte 2 bombers launched 19 raids against Moscow in October, mainly targeted at rail links to interfere with the movement of reinforcements. The Soviets estimated that attacks on rail connections typically caused halts in activity of five to six hours. Small numbers of Luftwaffe bombers were also dispatched against industrial targets to other Soviet cities. On October 5, three He 111 of KG 55 "Grief" attacked the large tank factory at Kramatorskaya, and the next night an arms factory at Rostov was attacked. Two weeks later, the same Staffel raided Aviation Plant 18 in Voronezh, a producer of Il-2s. On November 4, KG 2 and KGr 100 launched a raid against Gorky, 300km (186 miles) northwest of Moscow. The city was unprepared and 15 He 111s dropped incendiaries and high-explosive bombs at low

Soviet PVO fighters on patrol over Moscow. Moscow's 6 PVO IAK fighters struggled to intercept Luftwaffe bombers at night, and the lack of training in night operations led to 36 PVO fighters lost to landing accidents. (Courtesy of the Central Museum of the Armed Forces, Moscow via Stavka)

level. A factory producing T-60 tanks was damaged and no German aircraft were lost. A follow-on raid the next night met heavy antiaircraft fire from the now alert city and was the last raid against Gorky in 1941. On November 6, a particularly effective raid by 12 He 111s struck the railroad station at Yaroslavl, 250km (155 miles) northwest of Gorky, destroying 50 railroad wagons.

The first wet snow fell on October 5 while the bulk of Army Group Center was mopping up the Bryansk and Vyazma pockets. The *rasputitsa*, the fall rainy season, had arrived, turning the fields and unpaved roads to mud and making the Luftwaffe's improvised airstrips sodden and dangerous. The poor weather often limited air operations to only a few aircraft. As weather and the destruction of the pockets delayed von Bock, Marshal Zhukov was recalled from Leningrad to reform the Western Front, and thousands of civilians were mobilized to work on new defensive lines to protect the capital. Aviation reinforcements could be sent to the front more rapidly than ground forces, and Michugin's VVS Western Front received a new 77 SAD with SBs, Pe-2s, R-5 biplanes, and Il-2s along with the 177 Fighter Regiment from the Moscow PVO with MiG-3s and I-16s. The Western Front was rebuilt to a strength of 230–250 aircraft during October, and although obsolete Polikarpovs still made up 40 percent of the fighter force, for the first time, the VVS had large numbers of new-generation aircraft, including MiG-3s, LaGG-3s, and Pe-2s. Portions of the long-range DBA bomber force, which now had roughly 400 bombers in five divisions, were also sent to defend the capital. The 51 and 81 DBADs supported the West and Bryansk Fronts. DBA's DB-3s and TB-3s concentrated on night operations, while the Pe-2s, Pe-3s, and Yer-2s flew in daylight hours.

The defense of Moscow saw the largest-scale use of Il-2 Shturmoviks to date. Seven regiments – the 63, 74, 198, 214, 237, 243, and 299 Ground Attack Aviation Regiments – took part in the defense, and three more – the 312, 503, and 569 – joined in late October and November. Shturmoviks proved exceptionally effective at hitting German columns

A MiG-3 fighter prepares for operations in the snowy conditions on the Moscow front. VVS units were better prepared to operate in the freezing weather conditions encountered during the winter of 1941–42. (Getty Images)

Crowds view a German downed bomber put on display in Sverdlov Square in Moscow. Despite the setbacks experienced by the VVS, the Soviet leadership derived as much propaganda value as possible from any successes achieved by their airmen. (Getty Images)

stalled due to the mud, and unlike both sides' level bombers, were able to fly strike missions in low-cloud conditions and poor visibility. In the fall of 1941, Aviation Plants 16 and 32 began to fit RS-132 rocket projectiles under the wings of new-production Pe-2s. The rockets were heavier than the standard RS-82s and able to immobilize enemy tanks if they achieved direct hits.

Fighters from the 6 PVO Fighter Aviation Corps were sent to support the front after the disasters at Vyazma and Bryansk. It had 444 fighter aircraft when *Typhoon* began on September 30 and received the 28 Fighter Regiment with MiG-3s and the 436 with Yak-1s on October 13. The 208 Fighter Regiment joined the corps shortly after with Pe-2s used in the fighter role. The PVO pilots often had more flight hours than their VVS compatriots, and their aircraft were soon used in strafing and fighter-bomber missions over the front. Critically, some Soviet pilots began to use the two- and four-ship lead and wingman formations employed so effectively by the Luftwaffe, sometimes due to initiative, and at other times due to shortages of aircraft and pilots. These tactics would be fully adopted by the VVS in 1942.

VVS regiments continued to lose aircraft rapidly, with the poor training of Soviet pilots continuing to limit their effectiveness. Lieutenant Boris Kovzan of the 42 Fighter Regiment crash-landed after a taran ramming of a Bf 110, and when it was discovered that he still had half his ammunition, Kovzan confessed that he had not been trained to shoot accurately. The 126 Fighter Regiment overcame a different training challenge, as it was equipped with 12 Curtiss P-40 Tomahawk IIBs that arrived with the British Dervish Convoy on August 31 without manuals. The Soviet pilots were very impressed with the aircraft's cockpit layout and radios, but the low speed and poor climb rate led them to use war emergency power much more than recommended, shortening engine life. The unit flew 666 sorties in support of the Western and Kalinin Fronts and 319 in the direct defense of Moscow from October to April 1942, and claimed 29 victories for four losses.

Soviet airmen were now flying from well-equipped airbases in the Moscow area, while German ground-support staff were struggling to operate from improvised airstrips, which had turned to quagmires with the heavy fall rains, and at the end of a primitive line of communication hundreds of kilometers long. By the middle of October, the Soviets were often able to match or exceed Luftflotte 2's sortie rates, and on October 14 both the Germans and Soviets, unusually, reported equal losses – 12 each. Three of these were by JG 3 commander Major Günther Lützow, who increased his score to 97 by shooting down a TB-3, an LaGG-3, and a DB-3. The TB-3 was an unusual victory, as it was a unique version on a test flight configured to carry a piggyback unmanned fighter filled with explosives that was to be guided to its target by radio control. Six days later, Lützow would follow in Werner Mölders' footsteps, becoming the second fighter pilot in history to reach 100 kills.

Army Group Center outflanked Moscow's defenses to the north by seizing a bridgehead at Kalinin on October 13. The 81 Bomber Aviation Division flew 21 sorties against the city, claiming a direct hit by a FAB-500 on one bridge and a FAB-250 on another, but the Germans kept them operational. The Stavka reacted by forming a new Kalinin Front under General Ivan Konev on October 19 with the 22, the 29, the 30, and the 31 Armies pulled from the Western Front's northern flank. The commander of the 1 RAG, Colonel Nikolay Trifonov, was appointed VVS Kalinin Front commander, and received the 569 Ground Attack Regiment with 20 new-production Il-2s, followed within a few days by the 132 Bomber Aviation Regiment with 13 Pe-2s, as well as 17 MiG-3s, and 19 LaGG-3s in the 10 and 193 Fighter Aviation Regiments. The 6 PVO Fighter Aviation Corps and 81 Bomber Aviation Division were heavily committed to support Trifonov's small force.

Heavy wet snowfall and low clouds kept both air forces largely grounded on October 15, and the Luftwaffe and VVS reported seven losses each. On October 16, Luftflotte 2 was reduced to 241 sorties, while the 6 PVO Fighter Corps flew 330 and the VVS Western Front 291. Soviet aircraft repeatedly struck supply columns in Army Group Center's 9 and 4 Army rear areas, paying particular attention to the few heavily used hard-surfaced highways. With better flying weather to the south, Guderian's panzers, now formally redesignated the 2 Panzer Army, attacked towards Tula. Luftflotte 2 managed 458 sorties in support, and KG 53 "Legion Condor" suffered its highest one-day losses during the war, losing five crews and seven He 111 bombers. On October 26, poor weather completely grounded Kesselring's airmen, while the VVS Western Front flew 383 sorties, claiming hits on 148 motor vehicles and 33 tanks at a cost of ten aircraft lost. Two days later, Guderian's advance, now nearing Tula, led the Stavka to focus the 6 PVO Fighter Corps, VVS Western Front, 6 RAG, and 81 Bomber Aviation Division against his columns.

Soviet aviation strength, Moscow region, November, 1941		
	Total	Operational
Fighters	658	497
Bombers	423	203
Shturmoviks	46	28
Reconnaissance	11	10
Total	1,138	738

The Soviet airmen had played a major role in holding the line after the crushing defeats of Bryansk and Vyazma. By November, the VVS was outflying its opponents by a large margin. On November 4, the VVS Kalinin, Western, and Bryansk Fronts, along with

By the winter of 1941–42, Soviet forces began to transition to a large-scale counterattack that began against Army Group Center and was broadened by Stalin to cover the entire front. Here, a MiG-3 fighter regiment receives its elevation to the elite guards status. (Getty Images)

the 6 PVO Fighter Corps and 81 Bomber Aviation Division, flew 824 sorties while the Luftwaffe only flew 339. The next two days saw the Soviets fly 1,179 and 1,374 sorties, respectively. Losses were heavy, especially to Il-2 units, but were much less severe than earlier in the war, with a total of 293 aircraft lost from the start of *Typhoon* to November 5. Luftflotte 2's losses, for the first time, approached those of their opponents, with a total of 176 German aircraft destroyed and 67 severely damaged. Even though Moscow had yet to be captured, the Luftwaffe continued to withdraw units from the front. On November 11, Kesselring and his Luftflotte 2 headquarters and Fliegerkorps II's HQ departed to begin operations against Malta. Richthofen's Fliegerkorps VIII formally assumed control over the Luftwaffe assets remaining on the Moscow front on November 30. Soviet aviation totaled 1,138 aircraft on the Moscow front, outnumbering its opponents by a margin of over two to one.

Luftflotte 2 losses September 30–November 5, 1941			
Type	Total losses	Severely damaged	Total
Fighters	29	13	42
Bombers	68	12	80
Stukas	28	8	36
Ground attack	22	11	33
Army recon	23	19	42
Long-range recon	6	4	10
Totals	176	67	243

With temperatures plunging, the ground became frozen enough to support large-scale maneuvers by mid-November. Army Group Center resumed its offensive on November 17, but heavy snowfalls and below-zero temperatures followed a few days later. Unlike army leadership, Inspector General Erhard Milch had ensured that the Luftwaffe would be provided with adequate clothing for the winter, but the poor weather nevertheless reduced sortie rates. The airfields were often blocked with snow drifts, and starting aircraft engines in subzero temperatures was extremely difficult. Alert aircraft would have to be periodically started throughout the night hours, burning up precious fuel. One ground crew improvisation was the creation of "alert boxes," small sheds heated by ovens that could house and keep warm the nose and engines of aircraft. Even the mechanics' tools became brittle in extreme cold, and the ground crews had to warm them before working on aircraft. Locating their airfields in snowy conditions could be difficult for returning pilots, so ground personnel marked the runways with downed tree trunks. The Luftwaffe was typically operating from primitive field airstrips, or on former Soviet bases damaged in battle or by "scorched earth" measures. In contrast, many VVS units were able to operate from Moscow's well-equipped permanent bases, with hardened runways, hangars, maintenance buildings, and steady supplies of water and electricity.

While the winter weather made ground and air operations difficult, the frozen terrain allowed Army Group Center a renewed measure of mobility, and it again broke through Soviet defenses. The advance of the 3 Panzer Army and Panzer Group 4 to the north, and Guderian's 2 Panzer Army to the south, threatened to create a new, massive encirclement around the capital. Hoth's Panzer Army 3 posed the greatest threat, capturing Klin on November 24, although poor weather on November 23–24 limited air support. To the south, the weather was clearer, and the air assets left behind by Fliegerkorps II, now led by Nahkampfführer Martin Fiebig, flew in support of Guderian's tanks as they struck north. Unable to seize the city, Panzer Army 2 bypassed and partially encircled Tula as it advanced north, led by a battlegroup from the 4 Panzer Division.

Soviet ground forces were still outnumbered one to three in tanks, but the balance in the air continued to trend in the USSR's favor. Even during the final advance against the Soviet capital, the Luftwaffe continued to withdraw units. KGr 100 withdrew to Germany on November 13, and III./KG 4 was transferred north to Luftflotte 1 two days later. At the same time, the Soviets strengthened air assets at the key sectors. The 38 Fighter Regiment entered combat on November 16, flying British-provided Hurricanes alongside its MiG-3s. The Stavka dispatched a portion of the 6 PVO Fighter Corps south to help stop Guderian's 2 Panzer Army, and on November 25, assembled a new Air Group Petrov to combat Hoth to the north with 163 aircraft, 107 of them serviceable.

The German offensive ground to a halt in the heavy snows of late November, unable to overcome substantial Soviet resistance on the ground and in the air. On November 28, the 1 Shock Army, with Air Group Petrov in direct support, launched an attack against the 7 Panzer Division, with the 81 DBAD and 6 Fighter Corps joining in. The Soviets flew 771 sorties, while Richthofen only had 94 operational Bf 109s to cover the entire Army Group Center front. In the last ten days of November, Richthofen lost 38 aircraft in return for 44 victories. The last German attempt to advance on December 2 led to a major air clash, with the Luftwaffe claiming 29 kills and the Soviets 17, including the first victory by a 38 IAP Hurricane pilot. The VVS Western Front and 6 IAK PVO reported hits on 85–90 tanks and 149 other motor vehicles, and the roads began to be lined with destroyed trucks, wagons, and dead horses as German units pulled back from their exposed forward positions. On December 8, Hitler reluctantly issued a directive formally calling a halt to Army Group Center's offensive.

AFTERMATH AND ANALYSIS

Hitler's December halt directive for Army Group Center included orders for the Luftwaffe to accomplish a wide variety of tasks: supporting defending army divisions, severing enemy lines of communications, and striking Soviet armaments and training establishments as far afield as Gorky and Stalingrad. The orders were wildly ambitious given the departure of major Luftwaffe units in previous weeks and the difficulties of operating in winter conditions. On December 5, the reinforced Soviet fronts began their first winter offensive of the war. The VVS Kalinin, Western, and Southwestern Fronts and supporting fighters from the PVO's 6 IAK amounted to 1,393 aircraft, 910 of them operational, and faced less than half that number. The panzer armies on the flanks were driven steadily back during the month, with only the 4 Army in the center of the line able to adhere to the first Hitler "stand fast" order on December 16. For the first time, large numbers of Luftwaffe personnel – at times including highly trained pilots and maintenance specialists – were formed into ad hoc ground units and thrown into the line to fight as infantrymen. Richthofen informed Berlin that the situation had developed into a question of "to be or not to be," and soon Luftwaffe units were drawn from the west to reinforce the Eastern Front. Geim's Fliegerkorps V headquarters was ordered back from Brussels, where part of it would form a special staff for Crimea operations, while the other portion would form a Luftwaffe "Command East" to take over all support for Army Group Center in the Spring of 1942, as Richthofen and his Fliegerkorps VIII was sent south to support Army Group South's attack on Sevastopol and the Operation *Blau* offensive.

The first phase of the Soviet counteroffensive lasted 33 days and drove Army Group Center back from the gates of Moscow. The VVS flew 7,210 sorties during December in the VVS Western and Kalinin Front zones alone. Army Group North and Army Group South were also forced to evacuate their forward positions at Tikhvin and Rostov by Soviet attacks. The Red Army's initial success before Moscow led Stalin to order a massive, front-wide general offensive that pushed German forces to the brink of defeat, gained ground, but ultimately failed to attain the ambitious objectives set for it by the Soviet dictator. Leningrad remained unrelieved, and the attempt to encircle Army Group Center failed after months of intense

A formation of Ju 87s returning from a mission in October 1941. Aerial warfare on the Eastern Front was centered on support to ground operations, and so long as Bf 109s were available for air cover, the Ju 87 Stukas were some of the most useful Luftwaffe aircraft at the front. (Getty Images)

Destroyed Russian aircraft on an airfield taken over by the Luftwaffe, June 1941. (Getty Images)

combat. The Luftwaffe was able to launch a successful but costly airlift of supplies into surrounded German pockets at Demyansk and Kohlm throughout the winter months. Spring would bring a renewed Axis offensive in the south, Operation *Blau*, ultimately leading to Stalingrad and defeat in the winter of 1942–43.

By December, it was clear that despite inflicting huge losses, Operation *Barbarossa* had failed. Stalin's regime had survived, and Soviet ground and air forces were on the offensive along the entire length of the front, supported by a VVS that now outnumbered its Luftwaffe opponents. The Soviets had successfully evacuated their industrial resources to safety in the Urals and Siberia, and Lend-Lease aid from the Western Allies was beginning to arrive. The invaders' murderous and exploitive treatment of the populations overrun in the western USSR undercut any ability to mobilize support against Communist rule.

The Luftwaffe dominated the VVS in 1941 due to its experienced commanders, pilots, and ground staff, and its superior aircraft. The fighters and the veteran pilots inflicted huge losses on their VVS counterparts, but the Bf 109s suffered from high accident rates as the Luftwaffe advanced to unimproved airstrips deep in Soviet territory. The German twin-engine Heinkels, Dorniers, and Junkers were effective in attacking Soviet lines of communications, but they were frequently drawn into ground-support missions due to the limited numbers of Stukas and the small numbers of dedicated ground-attack Hs 123s and Bf 109 Es. The Bf 110s of ZG 26 and SKG 210, although only present in limited numbers, proved extremely capable in the ground-attack role during the campaign. The intense demand for ground support from 1942 onward led the Luftwaffe to centralize its Stukas and the fighter-bomber version of the Fw 190 into a more effective close-air support organization in 1943, while the medium bomber force increasingly waned in importance and virtually disappeared by 1945.

Soviet bombers striking a German artillery position. The VVS massed all possible support for the Yelnya counteroffensive against Army Group Center. The attack ultimately drove the Germans from the salient, but weakened the Soviet forces in the central region, and they would collapse rapidly when Hitler ordered the Operation *Typhoon* offensive against Moscow in the fall. (Getty Images)

The Luftwaffe was at the peak of its effectiveness during Operation *Barbarossa*, and the destruction of the huge Soviet VVS force in the western USSR in June was its major contribution to the campaign. With air superiority, the bombers and Stukas helped the army penetrate Red Army defenses and interdicted Soviet lines of communications. The crippling shortfall for the Luftwaffe in 1941 was its limited force structure, amplified by the vast theater of operations and ever-lengthening supply lines. The Luftwaffe had only a few thousand aircraft on the Eastern Front, and the pace of operations, accidents, and enemy action steadily reduced aircraft numbers and readiness. Like the Wehrmacht as a whole, the Luftwaffe struggled to supply units operating at the end of a line of communications that grew to be hundreds of kilometers long. The road network was primitive, the railroads had to be converted to the European standard, and there were too few Ju 52 transports to fly in more than a tiny fraction of the supplies needed at the front. Muddy and sub-zero fall and winter weather conditions worsened the situation, and the Luftwaffe's overall readiness declined from almost 70 percent in June to 40 percent in December. As a result, only a portion of the Luftwaffe's aircraft were operational on any given day, and its commanders were unable to meet the ground force's incessant demands for air support.

The Luftwaffe struggled to keep its airpower concentrated due to the length of the front, the limited number of aircraft, and the multitude of demands laid upon it. Richthofen's Fliegerkorps VIII was the only dedicated close-support formation in the Luftwaffe, and its support to Army Group Center played a key role in the initial victories at Minsk and Smolensk. Hitler's move of the unit to the north brought von Leeb to the gates of Leningrad, but the city was encircled rather than stormed. Richthofen's absence left Kesselring's Luftflotte 2 weakened and hard-pressed to both support Bock's defense at Yelnya and launch an air offensive against Moscow. In the south, the concentration of Luftflotte 4 airpower against the Uman pocket left little support for Reichenau's advance on Kiev or the Romanian siege of Odessa. Fliegerkorps IV was never able to dedicate enough aircraft to interdict Soviet naval operations in the Black Sea, allowing the Soviets to successfully support and then

Despite initial losses to the German Operation *Barbarossa* surprise attack that exceeded the total strength of the Luftwaffe in the East, the VVS was able to sustain operations against the German invasion throughout 1941, and by December outnumbered its opponents. (Wiki Commons)

evacuate Odessa and establish the sustained defense of Sevastopol, which did not fall until early 1942. Left without Greim's Fliegerkorps V after it was ordered to Brussels, Luftflotte 4 lacked the combat power to simultaneously support advances against Kharkov, the Donbas, into Crimea, and against the Caucasus. Early in Operation *Typhoon*, intended to be the decisive offensive against Moscow, the Germans weakened their air support at the decisive point by ordering the withdrawal of key headquarters, leaders, and over one half of Luftflotte 2's Gruppen.

Hitler ordered that Moscow and Leningrad be destroyed in early July, and explicitly ordered a bombing campaign against the Soviet capital on July 19. The Luftwaffe's bomber force in the east, however, was fully integrated into the Luftflotten and oriented to supporting ground operations, so a force had to be hastily assembled to be able to mount three 100-plus bomber raids. The large-scale raids on Moscow suffered few losses but inflicted little damage, and the bombers were drawn back to meet the pressing needs of the army at the front. The series of smaller-scale raids that followed were at best harassment operations. The Luftwaffe's September 8 destruction of Leningrad's food supplies had a devastating impact during the first winter of the siege and was probably the single-most strategically significant bomber action of the campaign. The ensuing raids on the city had less impact, and the 1,500 tons of high explosives delivered on Leningrad in all of 1941 would be matched by the RAF on a nightly basis during its campaign against German cities later in the war.

Although the VVS disappears from many accounts of *Barbarossa* after its devastating initial losses, it sustained operations throughout the campaign and challenged its Luftwaffe opponents daily. As with the Red Army, the *Barbarossa* offensive caught the VVS at a period of exceptional vulnerability. The force was in the midst of a major expansion and reorganization, and was saddled with large numbers of obsolete aircraft as well as a smaller number of new aircraft that few pilots were trained to fly. Tactics were outmoded, with the fighters still flying cumbersome 3-plane Vics, and most aircraft lacked full radio sets. The

Soviet factory assembling an Il-2 Shturmovik. By early 1942, the Soviet regime had survived the initial German onslaught, evacuated its industry to safe locations in the Urals and Siberia, and was fully mobilizing its society and economy for war. (Nik Cornish at www.stavka.photos/)

devastating purges of the late 1930s led to large numbers of underqualified personnel in command positions and a pervasive culture of fear and caution in leadership. The Luftwaffe's early smashing successes, along with the VVS's inability to execute the unrealistic orders from Stalin to destroy the attackers, led to a further series of reliefs, arrests, and executions, which only worsened the command turbulence in the early weeks of the war.

The arrival of units from other military districts, training units, and newly mobilized and equipped regiments allowed the VVS to continue the air war throughout 1941. The unceasing VVS efforts to attack ground units led to tensions between the German air and ground commanders, and many veterans' accounts of the first months of the war, including Guderian's, describe diving for cover due to low-level VVS attack runs. When German offensives shattered Soviet ground defenses, the Stavka often used its aviation forces to plug gaps in the line. After the destruction of Soviet aviation in the Baltic States, Novikov's VVS Northern Front and VVS Baltic Aviation arrived to slow Army Group North's advance on Leningrad. After the Kiev disaster, Soviet aviation delayed the German advance on Kharkov, allowing for the evacuation of industry from the city and the Donbas. During *Typhoon*, VVS, PVO, and DBA assets rushed to the front helped hold the line after the disastrous destruction of the Bryansk and Vyazma pockets in October.

The cost remained high, however, and Soviet airmen continued to suffer many more casualties than they inflicted throughout 1941. Apart from the new Il-2 and Pe-2 aircraft, Soviet bombers and fighters were outclassed by their German counterparts, and VVS regiments rapidly melted away in combat. The hasty training of Soviet pilots and aircrew made them easy targets for the Bf 109s, and the VVS still fragmented the control of its regiments between front and army headquarters. In air-to-air combat, VVS pilots suffered huge losses to their opponents. The obsolete SB bomber force was virtually eliminated, and while the new Pe-2 and Il-2 would be essential elements in the ultimate triumph of the VVS in 1943–45, small numbers and poor training and tactics limited their impact in 1941. The DBA attempted strategic bombing operations against Romania and Berlin, but the operations were small in scale and mostly significant for propaganda purposes. The sustained crises at the front led DBA bombers to be heavily committed to costly daylight ground-support operations. The obsolete TB-3s took heavy losses and would be confined to paratroop and supply transport roles, and the small numbers of new TB-7/Pe-8s had reliability problems and proved unable to launch long-range strikes against Berlin. DBA's DB-3s would soon be confined to night operations and would largely operate against targets close to the front and at night, even in 1945.

Measures were taken in 1941 to improve VVS operations, in particular the simplification of unit structures with the adoption of 30-strong regiments and two-regiment divisions, but Soviet airpower remained subordinated to armies, with only some divisions controlled at the front level. In 1942, Alexander Novikov, the new VVS Commander-in-Chief, instituted the creation of air armies to centralize the control of all aviation assets dedicated to the support of each front. 1942 would see other critical improvements, including the arrival of improved Yak-3, Yak-7, and La-5 fighters, the move to using the German 2- and 4-ship tactics rather than the cumbersome 3-plane Vic, and the fielding of more aircraft with full radio sets, allowing the VVS to fight their Luftwaffe opponents on more even terms. By 1943, the VVS was fully able to match the Luftwaffe and, by 1944–45, dominate the front.

Convinced during the planning for *Barbarossa* that Stalin's regime would crumble within weeks or months, the Nazi regime had made no preparations for the possibilities of a long war. German aircraft production numbers had been exceeded by Britain in 1940 and 1941, and even while evacuating its industry to the Urals, the USSR produced 15,000 aircraft to Germany's 12,000 in 1941. Nazi Germany was condemned to a sustained war of attrition that its military and economy were not prepared to wage, and with the US entry into the conflict in December 1941, the Luftwaffe would be doomed to fight outnumbered on multiple fronts for the rest of the war.

FURTHER READING

The campaign

Bergstrom, Christer, *Barbarossa: The Air Battle: July–December 1941*, Ian Allen Publishing: 2007.

Bergstrom, Christer, *Black Cross, Red Star: Air War Over the Eastern Front: Volume 1, Operation Barbarossa*, Vaktel Books, Sweden: 2021.

Erickson, John, *The Road to Stalingrad*, Harper & Row: 1975.

Forcyzk, Robert, *Moscow 1941: Hitler's First Defeat*. Osprey, Campaign 167: 2009.

Glantz, David M., *Operation Barbarossa: Hitler's Invasion of Russia 1941*. The History Press: 2011.

Glantz, David M., and House, Jonathan M., *When Titans Clashed: How the Red Army Stopped Hitler*, rev. edn, University of Kansas Press, Lawrence: 2015.

Hooton, E.R., *War Over the Steppes: The Air Campaigns on the Eastern Front 1941–45*, Osprey Publishing: 2016.

Kirchubel, Robert, *Operation Barbarossa: The German Invasion of Soviet Russia*. Osprey Publishing: 2013.

Kirchubel, Robert, with Komar, Gary, *Atlas of the Eastern Front: 1941–45*. Osprey Publishing: 2016.

Plocher, Generalleutnant Hermann, *The German Air Force Versus Russia, 1941*. USAF Historical Studies No. 153, USAF Historical Division, Air University: 1965.

Stahel, David, *Operation Barbarossa and Germany's Defeat in the East*. Cambridge University Press: 2011.

Stahel, David, *Operation Typhoon: Hitler's March on Moscow, October 1941*. Cambridge University Press: 2015.

Stahel, David, *Retreat from Moscow. A New History of Germany's Winter Campaign 1941–1942*. Farrar, Straus and Giroux: 2019.

Timin, Mikhail, *Air Battles Over the Baltic 1941*. Helion & Company: 2018.

The Luftwaffe

Bekker, Cajus, *The Luftwaffe War Diaries: The German Air Force in World War II*. Da Capa Press Edition: 1994.

Boog, Horst and Forster, Jurgen, *Germany and the Second World War: Volume IV: The Attack on the Soviet Union*. Clarendon Press: 2015.

Corum, James S., "The Luftwaffe's Army Support Doctrine, 1918–1941," in *The Journal of Military History*, Vol. 59, No. 1, January 1995, pp. 53–76.

Corum, James S., *Wolfram von Richthofen: Master of the German Air War*, University of Kansas Press: 2008.

Corum, James S., "Defeat of the Luftwaffe: 1935–1945," in Higham, Robin, and Harris, Stephen J., *Why Air Forces Fail: The Anatomy of Defeat*. University of Kansas Press: 2016.

Mitcham, Samuel W., *Eagles of the Third Reich: Men of the Luftwaffe in WWII*, Stackpole Books: Mechanicsburg, PA: 1988.

Muller, Richard, *The German Air War in Russia*, The Nautical & Aviation Publishing Company of America, Baltimore, Maryland: 1992.

Murray, Williamson, *Luftwaffe*. The Nautical & Aviation Publishing Company of America: 1985.

Neulen, Hans Werner, *In the Skies of Europe: Air Forces Allied to the Luftwaffe 1939–1945*, The Crowood Press, Ramsbury, Marlborough, Wiltshire: 2000.

Price, Alfred, *The Luftwaffe Data Book,* Greenhill Books, London: 1977 and 1997.

Rudel, Hans-Ulrich, *Stuka Pilot*, new edn, Black House Publishing, London: 2012.

Stanley, Colonel Roy M., *Looking Down on War: Eastern Front Images: Imagery from WWII and Cold War Intelligence Files*, Pen & Sword Aviation, Barnsley, Yorkshire: 2016.

Weal, John, *Luftwaffe Schlachtgruppen*, Osprey Publishing: 2003.

Williamson, Gordon, *Luftwaffe Handbook: 1935–1945*, Sutton Publishing, Stroud: 2006.

The VVS

Degtev, Dmitry, and Zubov, Dmitry, *Air Battle for Moscow 1941–1942.* Air World: 2021.

Drabkin, Artem, *Barbarossa & the Retreat to Moscow: Recollections of Fighter Pilots on the Eastern Front*. Pen & Sword, Barnsley, Yorkshire: 2007.

Glantz, David M., *Stumbling Colossus: The Red Army on the Eve of World War II*. University of Kansas Press, 1998.

Greenwood, John T. and Hardesty, Von, "Soviet Air Forces in World War II," in Murphy, Paul J., ed., *The Soviet Air Forces*, McFarland & Company, Inc., Publishers: Jefferson, North Carolina and London, 1984.

Hardesty, Von, and Grindberg, Ilya, *Red Pheonix Rising: The Soviet Air Force in World War II*, University of Kansas Press, Lawrence: 2012.

Jones, David R., "From Disaster to Recovery," in Higham, Robin, and Harris, Stephen J., *Why Air Forces Fail: The Anatomy of Defeat*. University of Kansas Press: 2016.

Khazanov, Dmitriy and Medved, Aleksander, *Bf 109E/F vs Yak-1/7: Eastern Front 1941–42*, Duel 65, Osprey Publishing: 2015.

Kozhevnikov, M.N., *The Command and Staff of the Soviet Army Air Force in the Great Patriotic War: A Soviet View*, University Press of the Pacific, Honolulu Hawaii: 2005. Reprint of 1977 edn.

Mellinger, George, *LaGG & Lavochkin Aces of World War 2*, Osprey Publishing: 2003.

Mellinger, George, *Soviet Lend-Lease Fighter Aces of World War 2*, Osprey Publishing: 2006.

Rastrenin, Oleg, *Il-2 Shturmovik Guards Units of World War 2*. Osprey Combat Aircraft: 2008.

Wagner, Ray, ed., *The Soviet Air Force in World War II: The Official History, Originally Published by the Ministry of Defense of the USSR*, Doubleday & Company: 1973.

Whiting, Kenneth R., "Soviet Air–Ground Coordination, 1941–1945," in Benjamin Franklin Cooling, ed., *Case Studies in the Development of Close Air Support*, Special Studies, Office of Air Force History, United States Air Force: 1990.

INDEX

Note: page numbers in bold refer to illustrations, captions and plates.

ace pilots 12, 16, 38, **44–45(43)**, 46, 52, 54, 69, 72, 84
air superiority 4, 11, 33, 89
air tactical formations 12, 13, 17, 25, 34, 39, **46**
aircraft 5, 14, 16, 23, **31**, 39, 52, 53–54, **57**, **83**, **88**
   AR-2 (USSR) **40**, 48
   Beriev MBR-2 flying boat (USSR) 53, 55, **56**
   Curtiss P-40 Tomahawk 56, 83
   DB-3 (USSR) 7, 13, 19, 23, **25**, 38, 43, 46, 47, **47**, **49**, 53, 66, 67, **71**, **73**, 82, 84, 92
   Dornier Do 17 **11**, 13, 14, 34, 39, 43, 64, 65, **65**, 88
   Fieseler Storch (Germany) 16, 59
   Focke-Wulf Fr 189 (Germany) 14, **53**
   Focke-Wulf Fw 190 (Germany) 24, 88
   Hawker Hurricane (UK) 16, 53, 56, **58**, 86
   Heinkel He 111 (Germany) 5, **10**, 13, 14, 19, 23, 34, 39, 50, 64, **64**, 65, 66, 76, **76**, 81, 82, 84, 88
   Henschel Hs 123 (Germany) **12**, 14, 42, 67, 77, 88
   Il-2 Shturmovik **11**, 12, 13, 23, 24, **24**, **52**, 72, 76, 77, 81, 82–83, 84, **84**, 85, 91, **91**
   Junkers Ju 52 (Germany) **13**, 14, 15, **60**, 68, 78, 89
   Junkers Ju 86P (Germany) 5, 16
   Junkers Ju 87 Stuka (Germany) **5**, 8, **8**, 12, 13, 14, 16, 19, 32, 35, 39, 42, 43, **46**, 55, **57**, 58, 64, 69, 72, 73, **77**, **78**, 80, **85**, **87**, 88, 89
   Junkers Ju 88 (Germany) 5, **11**, 13, 14, 22, 34, **38**, 39, **40**, 47, 48, 50, 55, 64, 65, **65**, 67, 68, 77
   La-5 (USSR) 24, **31**, 92
   LaGG-3 (USSR) 23–24, **24**, **31**, 64, **65**, 82, 84
   Messerschmitt Bf-109 (Germany) 4, 6, 12, 14, 16, 19, 22, **22**, 23, 24, 35, 38, 39, **40–41**, **44–45(43)**, 46, 47, **47**, 48, 51, 52, 53, **54**, 55, 56, 58, **59**, 65, 67, 69, 72, 76–77, 86, **87**, 88, 89
   Messerschmitt Bf-110 Zerstörer (Germany) 12–13, **34**, 35, 39, 48, 55, 69, **71**, 72, 83, 88
   MiG-3 (USSR) 5, 23, **24**, 34, **36–37(35)**, 38, 50, **50**, 51, 52, 56, 60, 64, **65**, 81, 82, **82**, 83, 84, **85**, 86
   Petlyakov Pe-2 (USSR) 24, **24**, 34, 35, 51, 72, 80, 82, 83, 84, 91
   Petlyakov Pe-8/TB-7 (USSR) 23, 66, **71**, 92
   Polikarpov I-16 Ishak (USSR) **4**, 19, **19**, 22, 35, 38, **40**, 51, 52, 53, 54, **55**, **65**, **71**, 72, 82
   Polikarpov I-153 Chaika (USSR) 22, **22**, 35, **36–37(35)**, 51, **64**, **65**, 76
   SM.81 (Italy) 16, 17
   Sukhoi Su-2 (USSR) 52, 72
   Tupolev SB (USSR) **11**, 23, **23**, 35, 38, **39**, **40–41**, 43, 46, **47**, 48, 51, 53, 55, 72, 82, 91
   Tupolev TB-3 (USSR) 19, 23, 47, 51, 53, **54**, **55**, 62, 78, 82, 84, 92
   Yakovlev Yak-1 (USSR) 24, 51, 64, **65**, 72
   Yermolayev Yer-2 (USSR) 66, **71**, 82
aircraft design 10, 12, 14, **19**, 22, **22**, 23, 24, 26, **31**
airfields 5, 6, 7, 9, **13**, 14, 24–25, 34, **34**, 35, **36–37(35)**, 38, 39, **40–41**, 42, 43, **43**, 48, 50, 57, **63**, **71**, **73**, 77, 81, 86, **88**

Alkanis, Yakov I. 26
antiaircraft defense 35, 46, **47**, **51**, **54**, 55, 59, 64, 65, 66, **73**, 82
ARR (Romanian Air Force), the 16, 39, 51, 52, 53
   GAL (Combat Air Grouping), the 16, 53
Astakhov, General Fyodor 50, 73

Balkan Campaign, the **11**, 14
barrage balloons **21**, 64, **66**, 69
Battle of Britain, the 16, 32
Bock, Generalfeldmarschall Fedor von 47, 64, 82, 89
Boldin, Gen I.V. 42
bomb loads 13, 14, **54**, **55**, 67, **73**
bombing raids 35–38, **36–37(35)**
   Berlin 7–8, 66, 67, **70–71**, **74–75(73)**
   Kassa 51
   Leningrad 67–69, **68**, **69**, 72, 90
   Moscow **64**, 64–67, **65**, **66**, 81, 90
   Romania 53–54, **55**
Budennyy, Marshal Semyon 7, 61, **77**

camouflage 5, 33, **73**
Chernykh, Gen Sergey 38
chronology of events 6–9
close-support missions 11–12, 14, **46**, 48, 51, 52, 81, 88, 90
CSIR (Italian Expeditionary Corps), the 16–17

Dietl, General Eduard 55

engines 5, 12–13, 17, **18**, 19, 23, 24, **31**, **50**, 66

Falaleyev, Gen F. Ya 7, **61**
Fiebig, Nahkampfführer Martin 86
fighter escorts 38, 43, **87**
Finnish Air Force, the 17, **17**
Flivo liaison officers 11
Förster, General der Flieger Helmuth 15
friendly fire 12, 58–59, 77
fuel and ammunition supplies 14, 15, **60**, 72, **73**, 78, 86

German strategy 4–5, 6, 7, 8, **8**, 11–12, 16, 31–33, **33**, 46, 47, 51–52, 55–57, 58, 62–64, **63**, 72, 76–81, 84, 85–87, 88, 89, 90, 92
German supplies to Axis allies 16, **17**
Göring, Hermann 10, 11, 17, **33**, 38, 64
Grauert, General Ulrich 15
Greim, General der Flieger Robert Ritter von 9, 16, 51–52, **81**
Guderian, Gen Heinz 6, 7, 8, **49**, 64, 69, 77, 78, 84, 86, 91

Halder, General Franz 33, 46, 64
Heer, the 4
Armies 51–52, 77, **78**, 80, 84, 87
Army Groups
   Center 7, 8, 9, 12, 13, 15, 46, 47, 48, 59, **63**, 64, 76, 77, **78**, 81, 82, 84, **85**, 86, 87, 89, **89**
   North 7, 8, 9, 32, 47, 48, **49**, **63**, 67, 68, 76, **78**, 87, 91
   South 7, 9, 16, **49**, 50, 53, **63**, 69, 73–76, **78**, 87
Corps 7, 47, 48, 55, 77
Divisions 6, 46, 48
Panzer Groups 42, **61**
   Panzer Group 1 8, 51–52, 72
   Panzer Group 2 6, 7, 8, 42, 46, **49**, **63**, 64, 69, 77, **78**, 80, 84, 86
   Panzer Group 3 7, 8, 42, 46, **49**, 77, 80, 86
   Panzer Group 4 7, 48, 67, 69, 76, 80, 86
Regiments

Luftlande-Sturmregiment 68
Paratroop Regiment 1 68
and structural evolution **79(78)**
Hero of the Soviet Union (award), the 26, 38, 50, 66, **71**, 72
Heydrich, Reinhard 52
Hitler, Adolf 7, 8, 15, 16, 19, 31, 32, **33**, 47, 62, 69, **71**, 76, 86, 87, 89, **89**, 90
   Führer Directive No. 21 5, 6, 32
   Führer Directive No. 33 64
Hoth, Generaloberst Hermann 7, 42, 46, **49**, 86
Hungarian Carpathian Corps, the 51

identification markings **36–37(35)**, 59
industrial evacuation 76, 88, **91**, 92
interdiction tactics **8**, 51, 58
Ionov, Gen Aleksey 47

Jeschonnek, General Hans 10, 31, 32, 33
Joppien, Capt Hermann-Friedrich 72

Kalinin, K.A. 26
Keller, Generaloberst Albert 8, **14**, 15, 32, **38**, 48
Kesselring, Generalfeldmarschall Albert 7, 9, **15**, 15–16, 32, 38, 42, 46, 62, 64, 65, **71**, 76, 77, 84, 85
Kiev pocket, the **77**
kill claims 12, **23**, 35, 38, 39, 52, 54, 56, 86
Kirponos, Gen Mikhail 33, 50, 51, 72, 73
Kokorev, Lt Dmitry 39–42
Konev, Gen Ivan 84
Kopets, Gen Ivan 5, 43
Kovsan, Lt Boris 83
Kuznetsov, General Fyodor 48

Leeb, Generalfeldmarschall Wilhelm Josef von 47, 48, **63**, 66, 67, 68, 76, 89
Lend-Lease aid 88
Leningrad siege, the 8
Loehr, Generaloberst Alexander 9, 16, 32, 33, 50, 51, 52, 68, 72–73, 76, 77
Loerzer, General der Flieger Bruno 7, 8, **15**, 16, 64
logistics 5, **13**, 14–15, 24–25, 42, 57, **60**, 77, 86, 89
losses 4, 6, 7, **10**, 15, 16, **25**, 33, 35, 38, 39, 42, 43, **43**, 47, 48, 50, 51, 52, 54, 56, 57, **57**, 64, 66, 67–68, 72, 73, **73**, **80**, 83, 84, **85**, 85
Luftwaffe, the 4, 5, 6, 7, **8**, 9, 10–11, 31–32, **33**, 57, 64, **80**, 85, 88, 89, 91, 92
   Aufklärungsgruppe ObdL (Reconnaissance Group) 5, 6, **6**
   Condor Legion 19, **19**, 22
   coordination with the Heer 11–12
   Fliegerkorps
     I 15, 67
     II 7, 8, 9, 11, 13, 14, 16, 46, 47, **63**, 64, 76, 77, **78**, 81, 85, 86
     IV 14, 16, 32, 38, 52, 54, **78**, 89
     V 9, 16, 50, 52, 72, 87, 90
     VIII 7, 8, **11**, 13, 14, 16, 32, **34**, 42, 46, **46**, **63**, 64, 67, 68, 69, 76, 77, **78**, 81, 85, 87
   Gruppen 9
   JG *(Jagdgeschwader)* 12, 17, 52
     JG 3 50, 51, 52, 84
     JG 27 43, 67, 81
     JG 51 35, 38, 39, **43**, 46, 69, 72, 76
     JG 52 52, 53, 76
     JG 53 39, 47, 52, 67, 76
     II./JG 53 **41**
     JG 54 39, **40–41**, 47, 48
   KG *(Kampfgeschwader)* 14, 17, 50, 77
     KG 2 **11**, 14, 43, 67, 81
     KG 3 14, 35, 64, 67
     KG 4 14

INDEX

III./KG 4 86
KG 26
 III./KG 26 64
 KG 28 65
 I./KG 28 64
KG 51 35, 50
KG 53 64, 65, 84
KG 55 14, 50, 76
KG 76 **40–41**, 69
KGr 100 81, 86
LG
 IV.(St)/LG 1 56
 LG 2 14, 67
Luftlotten 17, **18**, **57**
 Luftlotte 1 12, 14, 15, 32, 33, **38**, **40**, 48, 50, 57, 69, **78**, 86
 Luftlotte 2 9, 12, 14, 15–16, 17, 32, 33, 38, 42, 47, 57, 59, 64, 66, **71**, 76, 77, **78**, 80, 81, 84, 85, **85**, 89, 90
 Luftlotte 4 12, 14, 16, 17, 32, 50, 51, 57, 59, 72, 73, 76, **77**, 90
 Luftlotte 5 7, 13, 15, 17, 55, 56
SG/LG (*Schlactflieger*) 14
SKG 17
 SKG 210 35, 39, 69, 72, 88
Staffeln 17
 9./JG 54 **41**
 15.(Span)/JG 27 76–77
StG (*Sturzkampfgeschwader*) 17
 StG 1 13, **43**, 67, 72
 StG 2 8, 13, 67, 69
 StG 77 13, 35, 52, 77
ZG (*Zerstörergeschwader*) 17
 ZG 26 13, 34, **34**, 48, **71**, 88
Lützow, Major Günther 52, 84

maintenance and repairs 14, 15, 22, 57
map of air operations (June – August 1941) **49**
map of air operations (June – Dec 1941) **63**
Michugin, General Fyodor 38, 52, 77, 82
Milch, General Erhard 10, 86
military strength and complements 7, 10, 17, 19, 24, **28**, **29**, **30**, **40**, 50, 51, 57, **57**, 59, 61, 64, **64**, **65**, 69, 77, **79**, **84**, 85, 87, **88**, **90**
MKHL (Hungarian Air Force), the **9**, 16
Mölders, Oberst Werner 38, **44–45(43)**, 46, 81, 84
Murmansk operation 55–56, **56**, **57**, **58**
Mussolini, Benito **33**

Naumenko, Col N.F. 7, 43, **61**
Nesterov, P.N. 39
Nielsen, Oberst Andreas 55
night operations 11, **12**, 34, **39**, 53, 65, 66, 68, **74–75(73)**, **81**, 82, 92
NKSF (National Socialist Flying Corps), the **14**
NKVD, the 25, 26, **26**, 35, 38, 80
Novikov, Gen Alexander 7, **32**, 48, **49**, 55, 61, **61**, 67, 68, 91, 92

obsolescence 16, 23, 25, 60, 82, 90
Odessa siege, the 53–54, 72, 89–90
OKH (*Oberkommando des Heeres*), the 10, 33, 46
OKL (*Oberkommando der Luftwaffe*), 10, 32
OKW (*Oberkommando der Wehrmacht*), the 7
operational readiness 17, 24, 57, **59**, 89
Operations
 Barbarossa 4, 33, 88
 Blau (June – Nov 1942) 87, 88
 Typhoon (Sept – Oct 1941) 8, 61, **63**, 76–86, **78**, **85**, **89**, 90
orders of battle **18**, **27–28**

Pavlov, Gen D.G. 42, 46
performance 12, 13, 22, 23, **50**, 83
Pflugbeil, Generalleutnant Kurt 16, 52
Ploesti oilfields, the 16, 32, 52
Pokryshkin, Lt Aleksandr 52
POWs 80, **80**
production 11, 17, **17**, 19, 22, 23, 24, **24**, **31**, **50**, **52**, 60, **62**, 78, 81, 82, 83, 84, **91**, 92
propaganda 66, **71**, **73**, **83**, 92
Ptukin, Gen Yevgeniy 50
PVO (Homeland Air Defense) 5, 25, 61, 64, **65**, 66, **66**, 68, 69, **69**, **72**, 77, **81**, 82, 83, 84, 86, 87

radio communications 11, 12, 13, 25, 39, 42, **64**, 83, 84, 90, 92
RAF, the 32, 56, **58**, 67, **73**, 90
railway and infrastructural targets 9, 11, **41**, 47, 51, 55, 56, 58, 65, 69, 76, **76**, 81–82
ranges 13
recognition signals 59, 77
reconnaissance 5, 6, **6**, 14, 42, 48, 50, **53**, 58, **61**, 65, 66, 72, **73**, 80, **84**
Red Army, the 4, 12, 19, 26, 32, 58, 68, 73, **78**, 87
 Armies 7, 52, 80, 84, 86
 Corps 42, 43, 48
 Divisions 48
 Regiments 84
redeployments 81, 85
Reichenau, Field Marshal Walther von 51
reinforcements 4, 8, 33, 43, 46, 47, 48, 52, 59–60, 61, 64, **64**, 68, 72, 78, 81, 82, 87
Richthofen, General der Flieger Wolfram Freiherr von 7, 8, 16, 32, 42, 64, 67, 86, 87, 89
Richthofen, Hauptmann Johannes Freiherr von 34, **35**
Richthofen, Manfred von 16, **43**, 46
Romanian army, the 8, **49**, 52, 53, 54, 72
Rotte and Schwarm formations 12, 17, 39, 51
Rowehl, Oberst Theodor 5, **6**
Royal Navy, the 32, 56, **57**
Rudel, Hans-Ulrich 8, 69, 73
Rundstedt, Generalfeldmarschall Gerd von 7, 9, 52, **63**, 76
Rychagov, P.V. 26

Shestakov, Mayor Lev 53, 54
Smushkevich, Yakov V. 26, **26**
sorties 4, 6, 14, 16, 34, 39, 42, 47, 48, 50, 51, 52, 65, 67, 72, 77, 80, 83, 84, 85, 86, 87
Soviet Baltic Fleet, the 7, 8, **27**, **30**, 47, 48, **49**, 61, **61**, 66, **67**, 68, 69, **71**, 73
 Marat (battleship) 8, **63**, 69, **73**
Soviet Coastal Army, the 53
Soviet command organization 60–62, **61**, **62**, **64**, 77
Soviet Fronts 6
 Bryansk 8, **63**, 72, **77**, 78, 80, 84–85
 Kalinin 9, 84–85, 87
 Northern 7, 48, 55, 61, 91
 Northwestern 7, 20, 47, 48, 61
 Southern 20, 52
 Southwestern 8, 20, 50, 51, **63**, 87
 Western 7, 9, 20, 42, 43, 46, **46**, 47, 82, 84–85, 87
Soviet military purge, the 26, **26**, 91
Soviet strategy 5, 7, 33, 34–35, 38–42, 43, 46–47, **48**, **49**, 50, 51, 55–56, 59–60, 68–72, **73**, 76, 78, 83–84, **89**, 89–92
 and the Winter counteroffensive 9, **13**, **85**, 86, 87, **88**
Spanish Civil War, the 16, **19**, 22, 50, 77
Special Military Districts 25, 33, 34, **34**, 35, 38, **42**
 Baltic **40–41**, 48
 Leningrad **42**, 43
Speidel, General Hans 52, **54**
Stalin, Josef 5, 6, **6**, 19, 25, 26, **26**, 33, 34, 35, 50, 61, 66, 69, **71**, **85**, 87, 91
standard European rail gauge, the 14, 89
Stavka, the 7, 8, **20**, 59, 61, 72, 78, 80, 84, 86, 91
supply airlifts 88
Suprun, Stephen 60

Taiurskii, Gen Andrei 43
"taran" ramming attacks 39–42, 47–48, 66, 83
Timoshenko, Marshal Semyon 5, 7, 35, 46, 47, **61**
training and combat experience 10, 12, 15, 22, 24, 25, 26, 38, 47, 53, 61, 66, **80**, **81**, 83, 88, 91
Tripartite Pact, the 51
Trofimov, Col Nikolay 84
Tupolev, Andrei 26

Udet, Ernst 10, **43**
Ultra intelligence 65

Voroshilov, Marshal Kliment 7, 61, **61**
VVS (Soviet Military Air Force), the 4, **4**, 5, 8, 9, 19–20, **21**, 24, 26, 38, 39, 47, **51**, 58, 60–62, **63**, 69, **77**, **78**, 80, **83**, 86, 88, 89, **89**, 90, **90**, 91–92
 Air Group Petrov 86
 BAD (Bomber Aviation Division) 20, **20**, 84, 85
 BAK (Long-Range Bomber Aviation Corps) 46, 47, 48, 50, 51, **71**
 BAP (Bomber Aviation Regiments) 43, 55, 66, 72
 DBA (Long-Range Bomber Aviation) 6, 7, 8, 19, **21**, 23, **25**, **30**, 38, **39**, 43, 46, 47, **47**, 48, **49**, 50, 62, 66, **71**, 72, **73**, 77, 78, 82, 92
 DBAD (Heavy Bomber Aviation Division) **62**, **71**, 82, 86
 DBAP (Long-Range Bomber Aviation Regiment) 38, 48
 IAD (Fighter Division) 20, **20**, 43
 IAK (Fighter Aviation Corps) 61,**66**
 6 IAK 64, **66**, 77, **81**, 83, 84, 85, 86, 87
 IAP (Fighter Aviation Regiment) 35, **36–37(35)**, 39–42, 72, 82, 83, 86
 9 Guards Fighter (69) 8, **49**, 54
 modernization program 4, 19, 23, 24, 33, 92
 MTAP (Mine and Torpedo Aviation Regiment) 53, 66, **71**, **73**
 OSNAZ (Special Purpose Fighter Aviation Regiment) 47, 60
 and plans for expansion 24–25, 90
 SAD (Mixed Aviation Division) 5, 20, **20**, 34, 35, **35**, 38,39–42, **40–41**, 43, 48, 50, 51, 76, 82
 SBAP (High-Speed Bomber Regiment) 48, 53
 ShAP (Ground Attack Aviation Regiment) 82, 84

Waldau, General Hoffmann von 32
weaponry 12–13, 14, 22, 34, **35**,46, **51**, 59, **66**, 72, 83, 84
weather conditions 4, 9, 34, 55, **63**, 77, **78**, 82, **82**, 83, 84, 89
Winter War (1939–40), the 17, 19, 50, 72

Yelnya Salient, the 64, **89**
Yeremenko, Gen Andrey 69–72, **77**, 80

Zelyenko, Lt Yekaterine 72
Zhigarev, Gen Pavel 26, **32**
Zhukov, Marshal Georgy 9, 82
Zveno bomber weapon system, the **54**, **55**, **56**